MAXIMIZING
PROJECT VALUE

MAXIMIZING PROJECT VALUE

DEFINING, MANAGING, AND MEASURING FOR OPTIMAL RETURN

Jeff Berman

AMERICAN MANAGEMENT ASSOCIATION

New York • Atlanta • Brussels • Chicago • Mexico City • San Francisco
Shanghai • Tokyo • Toronto • Washington, D.C.

Special discounts on bulk quantities of AMACOM books are available to corporations, professional associations, and other organizations. For details, contact Special Sales Department, AMACOM, a division of American Management Association, 1601 Broadway, New York, NY 10019.
Tel: 212-903-8316. Fax: 212-903-8083.
E-mail: specialsls@amanet.org
Website: www.amacombooks.org/go/specialsales
To view all AMACOM titles go to: www.amacombooks.org

This publication is designed to provide accurate and authoritative information in regard to the subject matter covered. It is sold with the understanding that the publisher is not engaged in rendering legal, accounting, or other professional service. If legal advice or other expert assistance is required, the services of a competent professional person should be sought.

"PMI" and the PMI logo are service and trademarks of the Project Management Institute, Inc. which are registered in the United States of America and other nations; "PMP" and the PMP logo are certification marks of the Project Management Institute, Inc. which are registered in the United States of America and other nations; "PMBOK," "PM Network," and "PMI Today" are trademarks of the Project Management Institute, Inc. which are registered in the United States of America and other nations; ". . . building professionalism in project management . . ." is a trade and service mark of the Project Management Institute, Inc. which is registered in the United States of America and other nations; and the Project Management Journal logo is a trademark of the Project Management Institute, Inc.

PMI did not participate in the development of this publication and has not reviewed the content for accuracy. PMI does not endorse or otherwise sponsor this publication and makes no warranty, guarantee, or representation, expressed or implied, as to its accuracy or content. PMI does not have any financial interest in this publication, and has not contributed any financial resources.

Additionally, PMI makes no warranty, guarantee, or representation, express or implied, that the successful completion of any activity or program, or the use of any product or publication, designed to prepare candidates for the PMP® Certification Examination, will result in the completion or satisfaction of any PMP® Certification eligibility requirement or standard.

Library of Congress Cataloging-in-Publication Data

Berman, Jeffrey A.
    Maximizing project value : defining, managing, and measuring for optimal return / Jeff Berman.
      p. cm.
    Includes bibliographical references and index.
    ISBN-10: 0-8144-7382-2
    ISBN-13: 978-0-8144-7382-5
    1. Project management. I. Title.

  HD69.P75B49   2007
  658.4'04—dc22   2006016794

Printing number

10 9 8 7 6 5 4 3 2 1

THIS BOOK IS DEDICATED TO MY WIFE, ABBE,
AND MY DAUGHTER, RAICHEL, FOR THEIR NEVER-ENDING LOVE,
INSPIRATION, AND SUPPORT FOR WRITING THIS BOOK.

CONTENTS

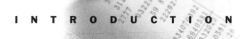

I N T R O D U C T I O N

BEYOND "ON TIME AND ON BUDGET"

What is project success? I always find the answer to this question interesting when speaking with different executives and managers across the country during my seminars and workshops. Most of the time, during these seminars, I get quick and confident answers back, often with many people simultaneously saying the same thing—"being on time and on budget"—as if they were part of a congregation or cult. The fact is that we have all been taught this simple rule of project management: Thou shall not be late and thou shall not exceed the project budget.

I got it. If I deliver my project on time and on budget, my boss will be happy (this is good), I will be considered a good project manager, hopefully get promoted (this is great), and the company overall is better off because the project I just completed was a success. All is good.

Now don't get me wrong, being on time and on budget is a good thing, but does this really mean that a project is successful? Is it possible that although a project is on time and on budget that the company is really better off? Perhaps the best way to answer these questions is to first define project failure. I can't tell you how many times executives have told me that their project(s) failed because the solution implemented

1

(whether a new technology, process, or organizational change) was not adapted to by the people affected by the project. These same executives tell me quite passionately that they have spent money (in some cases millions of dollars) with little or no result because the people just didn't adapt to the new change within the organization.

In the case of system implementations, this meant that the system users were not using the new technology and had gone back to manual processes or spreadsheets. In the case of process changes, this meant that department personnel and process owners were not adhering to the new policies and procedures. In any case, the bottom line is that the people went back to the old way of doing things after the change was implemented even though the project was on time and on budget. This means that the project objectives were not achieved and therefore no business value was obtained. Does this sound familiar?

Many of our projects today consume precious months (sometimes years) of time, allocation of resources (taking them away from doing other things), and a big budget that is spent with little or no gain. Of course, this doesn't account for the many projects that miss project timelines as well as exceed project budgets, making matters even worse. The fact is that failed projects, particularly the ones that provide little or no business value, cost companies millions of dollars each year. The result: lower profits, lack of business growth, and overall lack of competitiveness in the marketplace.

So what is business value? Business value can be summarized into four main categories:

1. Cost reduction
2. Business growth
3. Maintaining operations (e.g., regulatory compliance)
4. Speed and efficiency

A typical project will fall into one or more of these categories in regards to its overall objective. A project that is properly defined and executed should be linked to these business objectives from start to finish. This means that you as project manager must begin to change your mindset from tactically executing your project to strategically executing your project with these business objectives in mind. As such, project success becomes less dependent on the tactical execution of your project (being on time and on budget) and more focused on your project's ability to deliver business value. I look at it this way:

$$\text{Project success} = (\text{on time} + \text{on budget}) \times \text{business value}$$

Simply put, business value is a multiplier that increases the overall success of a project: The more business value that is achieved, the more successful your project will be. This means that even though a project is not on time and/or on budget, it can still be successful if project business value is achieved. Conversely, a project may be delivered on time and on budget and still be considered successful if no business value is achieved. In the latter case, however, project success is minimized because companies that deliver projects without providing business value will ultimately lose profits, lack business growth, and lose to the competition. It is the company that best utilizes precious time, money, and resources to achieve project objectives that will win in the end. As such, project business value becomes the key differentiator for delivering project success.

I believe that a project team spends at least 80 percent of their time implementing the solution. The solution may be a new system, a new process, or some other type of change that requires a new way of operating your business. The purpose again is to achieve one of the four business objectives mentioned above (reduced cost, business growth, etc.). Although most of our time and effort is spent on the actual implementation, I believe that only 30 percent of the business benefits will actually be achieved from just the implementation part of the project. The other 70 percent of the benefits will come from putting in place a process for making people accountable for the change and having a system in place for realizing the project benefits long after the project has been implemented.

This means that we as project managers have been taught and are still focused on just implementing the solution, which results in only 30 percent of the benefits. In many cases, even the 30 percent is never achieved. I believe this is because our mindset is solely focused on the tactical execution of being on time and on budget and not on the strategic business objectives that have been established at the onset of getting our project approved. Therefore, there is no link between the original business case of our project and the project value that is to be delivered by stakeholders after the project has been executed.

This is a fundamental flaw in our role as project manager, and it is a mistake for company executives not to ensure that this link is developed and delivered. "On time and on budget"—although still critical for project execution—is not a differentiator for business success and will not put your company ahead of the competition. Projects must go beyond "on time and on budget" to deliver business value, which I advocate as the new paradigm for project success.

Maximizing Project Value is the first book of its kind that provides a proven process for getting projects approved and maximizing project value. Through a step-by-step best practice approach for achieving project success this book will guide you through best practices and lessons learned from hundreds of projects at Fortune 500 companies as well as smaller companies focused on the multiplier of business value for achieving project success. The focus of the book will provide a proven *Speed2-Value*™ framework that will merge the tactical and strategic execution of a project by linking the original business case to realizable benefits after your project has been implemented. The result is a new paradigm for managing your project by establishing an ongoing project performance process that will achieve business objectives.

Maximizing Project Value is a "how to" book that will methodically guide you through this *Speed2Value*™ framework. We will start with learning how to establish a sound business case that can navigate the influential barriers and is both practical and defendable in terms of financial risk and reward. From establishing a solid business case you will learn to manage your project with business objectives in mind by developing project value drivers and Key Performance Indicators (KPIs) that will create an operational foundation for measuring ongoing project performance. From there, you will learn how to put in place a stakeholder management and communication process that motivates stakeholders to be accountable for results.

In the end, you as a project manager or company executive will be able to put in place an ongoing project performance process that will not only track ongoing performance, but will help ensure that what was approved in the original business case is actually being delivered. If you are like everybody else, project success is your goal. The difference is that you will now be armed with an ability to achieve project success by going beyond "on time and on budget" to maximize project value.

THE PROJECT *SPEED2VALUE*™ ROAD MAP

So how do you get business value from your projects? The answer is by focusing on executing a project from start to finish with maximizing project business value in mind. I call this the Project *Speed2Value*™ Road Map, as depicted in Figure I-1. Used on dozens of Fortune 500 projects large and small throughout the world, the Project *Speed2Value*™ Road Map is one of the most comprehensive approaches within the industry specifically designed to manage the full project life cycle and to track ongoing project performance.

Speed2Value™ was developed based on best practices from the Project Management Institute's (PMI's) *PMBOK*®, Six Sigma, Risk Management, Financial Management, and Change Management. The nice thing about the *Speed2Value*™ framework is that it can be used on all types of projects in all types of industries in conjunction with project execution methodologies, such as PMI's *PMBOK*®. The premise of

FIGURE I-1. The Project *Speed2Value* Road Map: The *Speed2Value* methodology is one of the most comprehensive approaches within the industry and is specifically designed for managing the full project life cycle and for tracking ongoing project performance.

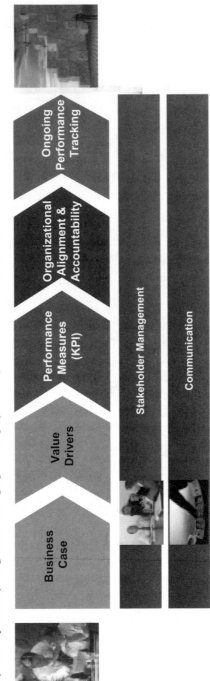

Speed2Value™ is based on three main ingredients that are required for project success:

1. *Buy-In for Your Project from Top Management.* Without the support from top management, your project will not be a priority and will ultimately compete for the resources required for executing the project, proper funding to implement it, and time needed to execute.

2. *A Clear Plan That Links the Original Project Business Case to Measurable and Ongoing Project Value.* Without a link to measurable project value, your project will just be another project that is executed on time and on budget without delivering a benefit to the company. Without a plan for obtaining project business value, it may be difficult not only to get your project approved, but to demonstrate that it is successful.

3. *A Process to Manage Change and Hold Key Stakeholders Accountable for Results.* As previously discussed, project success is determined by the ability of key stakeholders to adapt to the change or impact of the project. Without stakeholders adapting to change, the project will not deliver business value and will ultimately be considered a failure.

The starting point for achieving *Speed2Value*™ is to focus on developing a solid business case justification that clearly articulates a plan for delivering project success and therefore project business value. A successful business case will be the determining factor for getting your project approved and obtaining the required funding, resources, and time commitment from your company and executives. Leveraging off of the business case, the *Speed2Value*™ framework moves toward establishing "how" your project will identify and execute against business value drivers. Each of these value drivers show which financial drivers, business processes, and operational metrics will be used to drive the project results. From the point of identifying the project value drivers, key project performance metrics are established as a foundation for measuring project results.

After establishing these metrics, the organization is realigned so that accountability can be assigned. Once accountability is assigned, an ongoing tracking process is in place so that project results can be measured long after your project has been implemented. The true measure of project success is the point when your project is completed and when the true project results can be measured. This is where the ongoing business operations take over from the execution of the project. Without a process in place to adapt to the project changes as well as ensure accountability of results, project success will just be limited to being on time and on budget, without the means to measure business benefits.

In order to drive this entire *Speed2Value*™ process, the framework calls for the establishment of *foundation enablers*. These foundation enablers are the common thread that ties the original business case to the measurable project value to be achieved long after your project has been implemented. These foundation enablers are Stakeholder Management, Communication, and Project Risk Management. Without putting in place and managing these foundation enablers during the project execution, project success will be limited.

Buy-in from key stakeholders takes diligent and keen management through proper communication. As discussed above, without the buy-in from your project stakeholders, the business value will not be achieved. This is frustrating for the executives as well as wasting a lot of time, money, and resources of the company. The end result is exposing your company and project to unnecessary business risk. Business risk could be ultimately avoided if properly managed throughout the duration of the project. By establishing these foundation enablers as pillars to your project, success—defined as achieving real business value—will be the ultimate result. Through the remaining chapters of this book we will explore each dimension of the Project *Speed2Value*™ Road Map and how it can be used as part of your overall project implementation plan. Using this framework will be the difference between getting beyond "on time and on budget" to delivering real project success in terms of achieving overall project business value. We will use the *Speed2Value*™ framework throughout this book as a step-by-step guide for maximizing project value.

CHAPTER 1

DEFINING THE PROJECT BUSINESS CASE AND GETTING BUY-IN FROM TOP MANAGEMENT

The first step in the Project *Speed2Value*™ Road Map is to develop a project business case. In doing so, you as project manager will begin to lay the foundation for achieving project success by obtaining buy-in from top management and getting your project approved. This means getting the powers at large to give you the required funding, resources, and time to execute the project. Sound simple? It is not by a long shot. With chief executives mandating tighter control over spending, financial support for projects comes at a premium. Resources are limited at best, and there is not enough time to do all things necessary to keep the business running smoothly. If you are like the rest of us, I am sure you have put in your fair share of working more than eight hours in a day, weekends, and holidays on occasion. Am I right?

With that said, I am sure that you are not the only one in your company with limited time or a good idea for a project. It is a given that every proposed project out there is in competition for the same re-sources, limited funding, and time to be spent for implementation.

Therefore, it is up to you to justify that your project is better than the rest of the proposed projects so that you are one of the few winners for getting the limited resources, funding, and time commitments from the powers that be.

The key to getting your project approved is your ability to prove that your project, among all others, will deliver business value to the company. This means that you must be able to articulate "how" your project will deliver one or more of the main business drivers: cost reduction, business growth, maintaining operations (e.g., regulatory compliance), and increasing speed and efficiency. Keep in mind that these business drivers are why projects are executed. These are the drivers that keep your company profitable and keep your company competitive, and you must demonstrate how one or more of these business drivers can be achieved by your project in order for it to get approved. This is the premise for putting together what is called a project business case.

In simple terms, a *project business case* is a project justification document that outlines a project proposal and plan for authorized funding, resources, and implementation. It is a plan for execution and more importantly a plan for achieving project business value. The objective of a project business case is to justify:

- *What* benefit and cost the project brings to the business
- *Why* the project is important and should be funded
- *Where* the project needs to be implemented
- *When* the project can be implemented
- *Who* is required to implement the project
- *How* the project can be implemented with success

A business case is typically mandated by organizational policies and management preferences. The key is that the business case is used to approve a project as well as to serve as a baseline for determining project success. Think of the business case as your first benchmark for your plan of action as well as a measure for success. If all goes right and your project is approved, you will be on your way toward laying the foundation for building a project success plan of action.

Like a blueprint for building a house, a business case is the blueprint for achieving project success. Would you want your house built without a plan? If you are going to invest hundreds of thousands of dollars, I'm sure you would want to know what the plan is:

What type of house is it (3 bedrooms or 4)?

Why does it cost so much?

Where is it going to be located (facing north or south)?

When will it be built?

Who is building it (are they reputable)?

How will the house serve me and my family for the future to come?

Wouldn't you agree that you would have to know the answers to these questions before deciding whether to spend your hard-earned money on building the house? It's the same with the business case for a project, but instead of it being your hard-earned money, it is your company's. Instead of you and your family living in the house for the future to come, it is your company and all of its employees who will be affected by the project you are proposing. As such, the business case is the blueprint for success; it is the plan for a project that will best serve company employees and help make your company more profitable and better off by its implementation. It is therefore up to you to articulate the case why your project will serve the company best and how you plan to make it happen.

A business case can look different from organization to organization; however, the key components remain the same. All of the basic questions must be answered (who, what, when, where, why, and how). I frequently get asked, "Do all projects require a business case?" The quick answer is yes, although some business cases are more formal than others. For instance, a small project, such as deploying six new laptops for the marketing group, may only require a purchase order and an e-mail committing resources from the Information Technology department.

However, the thought process for approving the small project is the same as for approving a larger project. *Who* needs the laptops (everyone or just a few people in the department)? *What* types of laptops are required (as you know there are many to choose from)? *When* do the laptops need to be purchased and to be in the hands of the marketing people? *Where* will the laptops be used? *Why* are laptops even needed? *Why* can't they use desktop computers like everyone else? *How* will the laptops be deployed? I am sure you get the picture. The point is that no matter how small the project, the thought process is the same as long as funding, resources, and time are involved. More than likely this will be the case most of the time.

Most projects, however, require a more formal type of business case, because they require more funding, resources, and time to implement. By formal, I mean a well-documented report that clearly articulates the answers to all of the questions (who, what, when, where, why, and how). A good rule of thumb is that the larger the proposed project, the more time is required for formalizing a business case.

Information Technology projects are the most common projects requiring business cases. These may include projects related to networking, application systems, system integration, reporting, technical infrastructure, or software development. Other types of projects may include research & development (e.g., new products or pharmaceuticals); implementing new processes (e.g., reengineering the work flow of the supply chain); organizational restructuring (e.g., a merger of two companies or departments); construction, design, and engineering (e.g., highways, facilities, housing); and many, many more. Basically, projects ranging from thousands to many millions of dollars require a business case as long as they are competing for the same business constraints (time, money, and resources). The bottom line is that the business case can serve as the formalized document for getting your project approved as well as a baseline for measuring project success.

BUSINESS CASE PROCESS LIFE CYCLE

Most people don't think much of a project business case, let alone think that there is actually a process that a project business case goes through in order for it to get approved and succeed in delivering measurable business benefits. Getting a project approved takes effort, thought, and finesse. A project business case is a way to help achieve the goal of getting your project approved. It follows it's own sequence of steps or phases before it is approved. This is what I call the business case life cycle, or sequence of steps (see Figure 1-1).

STEP 1: DETERMINING THE NEED FOR A PROJECT

The first step of the business case life cycle is determining the *need for a project*. Needs for a project can be driven by a market need, such as a new product that will fill a certain void in the marketplace or a new elementary school to be located in a new master plan community. There may also be a business need, like a new software application that will help in productivity or efficiency of the workforce or a new restaurant to be built to service a community. Regulatory or legal need is also a driver, such as compliance with a financial filing or the advocacy of a product to be used on humans (e.g., drugs and medical devices).

Of course, the need for a project may derive from a simple stakeholder request, whether it is a customer change to a product or a taxpayer requesting the widening of a highway to help handle traffic due to population growth. Last but not least, a need for a project may be driven by a technological advancement, such as new manufacturing equipment or computer and phone networks to enhance communication. The bottom line is that the need for a project may come from many different places and at different times from different people or organizations, or even just from an idea that you developed. Without the need for a project, there is no reason to pursue getting resources, time allocation, or money.

FIGURE 1-1. Business case life cycle: need for a project.

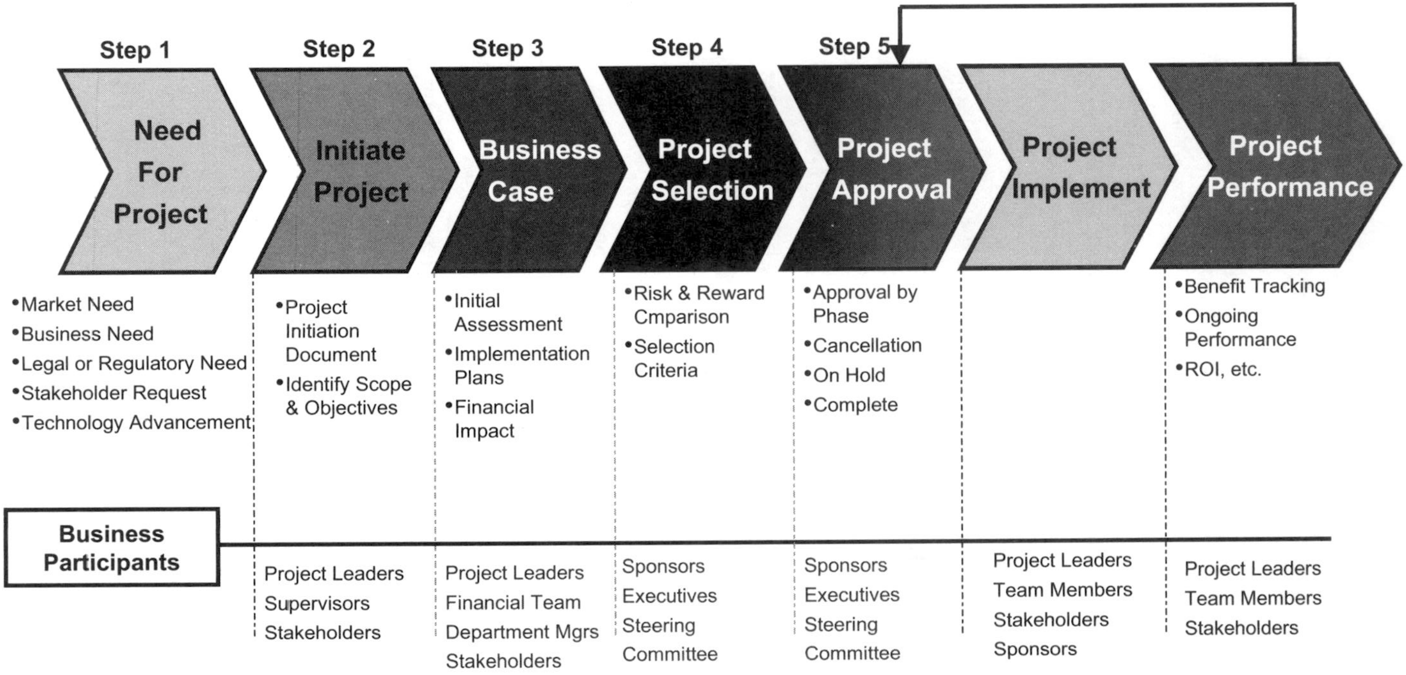

STEP 2: <u>INITIATING THE PROJECT</u>

Once the need is determined and it is deemed an idea to pursue, the project should then be *initiated*. This is the second step of the business case life cycle. Sometimes a project initiation comes from you just asking your boss for the verbal approval to pursue a project in terms of developing a business case. Other times, a formal request is required to be filed so that a committee or council can approve the need for a detailed analysis or formal business case. For the larger and more formal type projects, this initiation is what I call the *Project Initiation Document,* or PID (see Figure 1-2). This is a document that begins the business case development process by formally documenting the project objectives and description; leadership and organization; and overall project scope.

Objectives and Description

The first component of the PID is the "Objectives and Description" section. Basically, this is the "what" and "why" you want to obtain funding and resources (see Figure 1-3). Within the objectives and description section is the unique project identifier. Typically this is the project identification number or project code most likely assigned by the accounting department or cost accounting system. This number can be randomly assigned, or in some cases is a "smart" number whereby the codes within the number are defined to mean different things, like department or cost center.

For example, in the project code "00301CAP," "003" might stand for public works department, "01" for January, and "CAP" for capital project. The idea is that many companies may have many different unique identifiers or project codes particular to their organization. The only rule of thumb is that the project number be unique for the purposes of being tracked and accounted for once it is approved.

The second part of the "Objectives and Description" section of the PID is the project description itself. Typically this is a short text description of the project such as, "Deer Valley Elementary School Building"

(text continues on page 18)

FIGURE 1-2. Project Initiation Document (PID).

Based on determined needs for a project, a Project Initiation Document (PID) should be put together for obtaining initial approval to work on a formal business case.

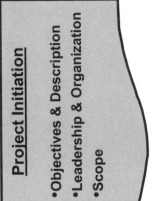

Project Initiation

- **Objectives & Description**
- **Leadership & Organization**
- **Scope**

Need for Project

- Market Need
- Business Need
- Legal or Regulatory Need
- Stakeholder Request
- Technology Advancement

FIGURE 1-3. Project initiation: Objectives and Description.

To initialize a project, typically an organization requires a unique identifier and a project description along with two main objective categories.

■ **Project Identifier:** Typically a unique project number or an assigned account number.

■ **Project Description:** A short text project name that describes the project.

■ **Business Objective:** Identifies the main business objective on which the project will have an impact. Although many organizations have unique and specific business objectives related to their business, typical business objectives include:

　– Cost Reduction

　– Revenue Growth

　– Maintaining Operations (e.g., regulatory compliance)

　– Speed and Efficiency

or "SAP Software Implementation." The key is that it is short and sweet and gets to the core of what the project is about. Think of the project description as something that would describe the project in a nutshell to someone with little knowledge about the details of your business.

Next describe your business objective or what your overall mission of the project is going to be. Typically this would include cost reduction, revenue growth, maintaining operations, and achieving speed or efficiency. The business objective is critical to establishing the foundation for why it is important that funding and resources are to be obtained for this project.

Leadership and Organization

The second component of the PID is "Leadership and Organization," or *who* will be involved with leading the project. Within this section, you should describe the project leader, project sponsor, and project category (see Figure 1-4). The *project leader* is typically a project manager who will be responsible for managing the daily activities and implementation of the project during the project life cycle implementation. The *project sponsor* is typically a senior level manager who will oversee the project implementation and be responsible for ensuring that business risks are mitigated and the project will be successful.

The *project category* is where the project belongs within the organization of project portfolios. Many organizations have unique and specific project categories related to their business. Examples of projects within an IT organization may include application systems (such as human resources, accounting, enterprise resource planning [ERP], and supply chain); data and information (e.g., data warehouse, reporting, development); infrastructure (e.g., desktop, hardware, networking, telecommunications); operations and services (e.g., manufacturing, training, knowledge management, Internet). Another example may be projects within a state agency; projects of the Department of Transportation might include research, highway design, construction, and maintenance. Within each one of these categories you may have more granular level

FIGURE 1-4. Project initiation: leadership and organization.

The Project Initiation Document should include the determination of the project leaders, sponsors, and categories.

- **Project Leader:** Typically a project manager who will be responsible for managing the daily activities and implementation of the project during the project life cycle.

- **Project Sponsor:** A senior level manager who will oversee the project implementation and be responsible for ensuring that business risks are mitigated and the project will be successful.

- **Project Category:** The category that the project belongs to within the organization of project portfolios. Many organizations have unique and specific project categories related to their business, however, typical categories include:

  - Application Systems (e.g. HR, accounting, ERP, supply chain, etc.)
  - Data & Information (e.g. data warehouse, reporting, development, etc.)
  - Infrastructure (e.g. desktop, hardware, networking, telecommunications, etc.)
  - Operations & Services (e.g. manufacturing, training, knowledge management, internet, etc.)

categories: for construction, for instance, you might have highways, roads, and bridges.

The point is that categories need to make sense to the organization and that they should be defined at the corporate or enterprise level so that every project that is initiated is classified into one of the already predefined categories. In the end, the organization will be able to review a portfolio of projects and be able to properly assess which projects and how many of what type to approve for funding and resources.

Project Scope

The third and perhaps most critical component of the PID is the "Project Scope" (see Figure 1-5). The Scope is the basis for putting together all of the details required for the detailed business case document and provides a way for executives or readers of the PID to get their hands around the project by sensing how big it really is. Within the Scope section of the PID the following items should be discussed:

Project location

Project business units or organizational departments

Stakeholder departments

Project milestones

Project approvers

The *project location* describes the location(s) where the project will be implemented. Typically this can include manufacturing plants, facilities, regions and/or countries. *Project business units* are defined as strategic operating units of the business, or a unit of the business that has its own profit & loss statement. A stakeholder is someone or a group of people that will be affected by or that can have an impact on the project, either positively or negatively.

Stakeholder departments are the departments or organizational units to which key stakeholders belong and which will be affected by this project (e.g., accounting, manufacturing, construction). Stakeholder

FIGURE 1–5. Project initiation: project scope.

Scope is one of the key elements for initiating a project. This will be a key input to developing the business case details.

- **Project Location:** The location(s) where the project will be implemented. Typically this can include plants, facilities, regions, and countries.

- **Project Business Units:** A strategic operating unit of the business or a unit of the business that has its own Profit & Loss statement.

- **Stakeholder Departments:** The department to which key stakeholders belong and which will be affected by this project (e.g., accounting, manufacturing).

- **Project Milestones:** The key project stages for the project life cycle (e.g., Initiate, Plan, Execute, Monitor, Close).

- **Project Approvers:** The organizational role that is required to approve the project at each project stage or milestone (e.g., IT director, CIO, VP operations, accounting manager, plant manager).

units can also include external customers, neighborhoods/communi-
ties, or government agencies. Identifying a stakeholder group or unit
is key to the overall scope of the project because they may have an
impact on the project one way or the other by increasing or mitigating
the overall project risk and the probability of success. If, for instance,
a stakeholder group identified includes the accounting department and
we know that accounting never wants to change their way of doing
things, this may jeopardize getting your project approved unless you
have a clear and well-thought-out plan to mitigate the risk invoked
by this group.

Project milestones are the next important element of the scope. Milestones include the key project stages for the project life cycle implementation (e.g., Initiate Plan, Execute, Monitor, Close) along with dates and
duration (length of time to complete each stage). The milestones provide
a view of the high-level activities that will be accomplished by the project, along with key dates. This high-level timeline provides executives a
quick view of when the project will be completed.

The last part of the scope is identification of the *project approvers*. Typically this will include the organizational role that is required to approve
the project at each project stage or milestone (e.g., functional manager
or department head, accounting manager, director). Typically the overall
size and complexity of the project will determine how many and which
approvers will be required. It is important to identify accountability for
approving the project upfront so that the approval process does not increase the overall duration of the business case life cycle. This will help
avoid the statement of, "good project idea, but I am not sure who needs
to approve it" syndrome.

The PID is a good document for beginning the thought process required for detailing out the business case. It should not take very long to
put together and is a good way to get your thoughts down to see if your
idea is really worth pursuing in terms of the effort in putting together a
business case.

STEP 3 : MAKING THE BUSINESS CASE

Once the PID is completed, the detailed business case development can begin. The business case document is made up of three components (see Figure 1-6):

1. Initial Assessment
2. Project Implementation
3. Financial Impact

Within each of these components, several topics are addressed. Many of the topics under Project Implementation and Financial Impact are part of the overall project selection criteria that an approver goes through in order to make the final decision of whether your project gets approved or not. We will discuss the selection criteria as part of the *business case influencers and supporter section* later in the chapter. For now, let's focus on the Initial Assessment components of the business case (see Figure 1-7).

Initial Assessment

In order to properly assess a project for its merit, we must first look at the current situation of the environment for why the project is needed. This is part of the initial project assessment. Some call this "pain points," others call it "the need for change." Basically, you should describe what is currently working well within your business and what is not working so well.

By focusing on what is not working so well, you should then describe the impact of the current situation in terms of the "pain point" or the "need for change." Discuss things like loss of productivity, low customer satisfaction, high inventory, employee turnover, and low morale. In addition, talk about your competitors. Relate the need for change in terms of what will be lost to competitors if action is not taken. For example, "If we do not take action to address our current pain, then we will lose market share to Company Xtron, our largest competitor." Loss of market share,

(text continues on page 26)

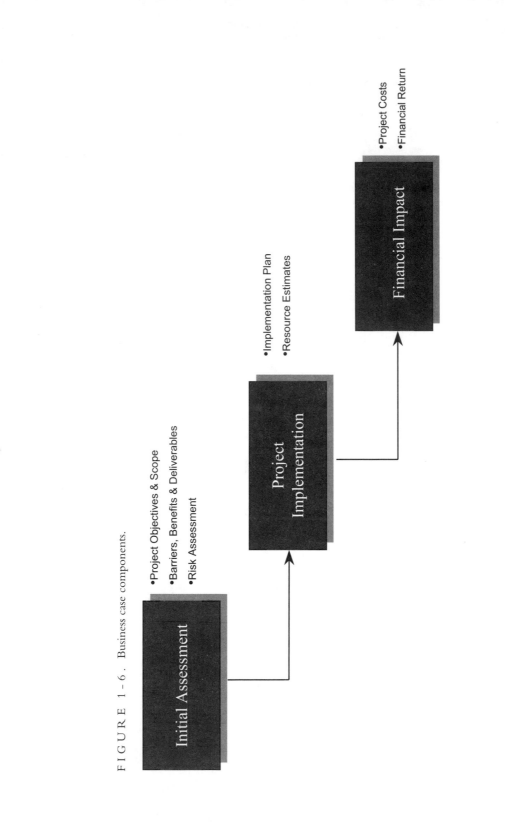

FIGURE 1-6. Business case components.

Initial Assessment

•Project Objectives & Scope
•Barriers, Benefits & Deliverables
•Risk Assessment

Project Implementation

•Implementation Plan
•Resource Estimates

Financial Impact

•Project Costs
•Financial Return

FIGURE 1-7. Initial assessment components.

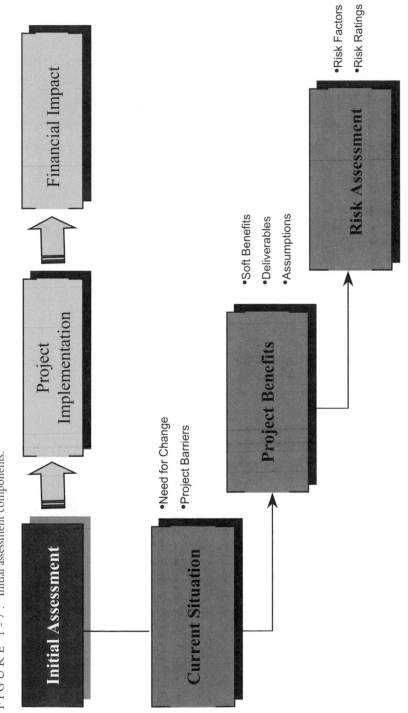

customers, profit margins, and good employees are all costs to the business that magnify the impact of not changing the current situation.

In addition to the need for change, the project barriers should also be described within the section on "current situation." *Project barriers* are things that would impede your project from being successful, such as, for example, project location. Say that your project is the construction of a new building in the center of the city. Implementation or construction of the building may cause major issues regarding traffic and logistics for getting equipment to the job site. The result may be delays or additional costs for equipment and permits.

What about the type of project you are proposing? What if this is the first time a project of this nature has ever been done within your organization? This would certainly be a barrier. Your project may also require certain kinds of resources, such as special skills or security clearances for government-related work. Another type of barrier may be the timing of the implementation in relation to business cycles, such as when you are proposing to implement a project during the peak selling season, when resources are scarce. These could all be potential barriers for your project.

In order for your project business case to be credible, it is always a good idea to share your concerns about true barriers openly. As a rule of thumb, if you don't do a good job thinking through some of the issues, then you will not be prepared enough to answer the right questions to overcome the "nay-sayers" who have the authority to approve or deny your project. Be prepared and be honest. It will go further than you think. In the next section we will discuss the Project Implementation and Financial Impact components of the business case. These will be major parts of the project selection criteria discussion, which is the second key influencer to getting your project approved.

BUSINESS CASE INFLUENCERS AND SUPPORTERS

I would be lying to you if I told you that just putting together a solid business case is all that it takes to get your project approved. Like anything in this world, there are always gray areas for getting things done. Getting your project approved is no different. A good business case also considers that there are influencers and supporters who must come in line to get the job done and approve your project for implementation. Make no mistake about it, your ability to navigate between your business case influencers and supporters may be the difference in getting your project approved or having it passed over for some other project. Understanding these influencers and supporters is the key to your success, and your ability to leverage these influencers and supporters throughout the business case life cycle is your silver bullet for obtaining approval (see Figure 1-8).

Influencer #1: Politics

No matter how big or small your project, politics will always come into play for getting your project approved. Whether it is your boss looking for a promotion or his peer competing for the same funding, somebody, somewhere, will have an agenda that could derail all of your hopes and dreams for getting your project approved. Over my twenty-plus-year career in working with many Fortune 500 clients as well as smaller ones,

FIGURE 1-8. Business case "influencers."

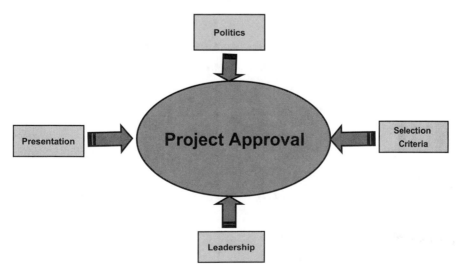

this unfortunately has always been the case. The important thing is to understand this and to incorporate what I call "political mitigation" into your overall plan for building and selling your project business case.

Political mitigation is based on understanding who the players are for approving your project. Who needs to formally sign off on your project? Who influences those who need to sign off? What are the possible road blocks that can cause your designated approver to not approve your project? Depending on how large your proposed project is, in terms of required resources and funding, your proposed project may have up to five different approvers. For a typical IT project, there are three approvers, consisting of the chief information officer (CIO), the chief financial officer (CFO), and the head of the department from where the actual budget will come. Other types of projects may just have a department head and a financial controller or CFO. In some cases, again depending on the size of the project, the chief executive officer (CEO) as well as the human resource (HR) director may also be involved in approving the project.

Depending on the size of the organization, the approver may not always be at the executive level, but will most likely include, at a minimum, the appropriate department head and a designated director-level person from finance. In some cases project approval will come from independent signatures that flow from one approver to the next. In other cases, an executive committee is formed that has the sole purpose of approving projects and overseeing them for success. In any case, project approval typically comes from an executive level within the organization. The higher the proposed project budget, the higher up in the organization you must go for approval.

Now depending on which department you work for, your access to this level of approver may be limited. But don't panic, all is not lost. The fact is that because of pressures of time and the scope of their job many people at the executive level rely on information from others within the organization for making decisions. These people, called influencers or "go to" people, have proven expertise and knowledge, and they enjoy the respect of people at the executive level. Most of the time, go-to people have informal access to executives and are able to provide them with a sense of what is really happening in the organization and/or the detailed knowledge for making a decision.

Every executive has such individuals, whether a formal right-hand man or woman or informal confidant. Having such individuals is a must in order for executives to survive the day in and day out climate of normal business operations. Therefore these go-to people are the ones that can make or break your business case approval, because they are the ones that offer the most influence to the decisions made at the top. The good news is that getting to these people may be a lot easier for you to state your case. The bad news is that each of these individuals may come with different agendas that may not align with the objectives of your project and therefore may produce a negative outcome for getting your project approved.

Each agenda offers a potential road block that must be navigated around in order for you to be successful. Say, for example, you are proposing to implement a software application that is in conflict with an existing application being used by Charlie, a go-to person for the CIO. Do you think Charlie will endorse your project or will he put up a road block for getting your project approved? In another example, let's look at Sally, a supervisor for the design team within the research & development (R&D) department and go-to person for the R&D department head. Assume your proposed project requires two critical resources from Sally's design team at a time she already has scheduled to deliver her new product designs to a key client. Do you think Sally will endorse your project or will she become a road block for getting your project approved?

These are two simple but common examples of road blocks that are caused by different agendas that are critical to the go-to person. The idea here is that it is up to you to identify these different agendas so that the road blocks can be removed or negotiated for the purpose of getting your project endorsed. In the case of Charlie, perhaps you can meet with him before your business case is submitted to show him how your new software application can help him and his team save time and effort and that it does not really conflict with his existing application. Or in the case of Sally, perhaps you can agree on a time frame for utilizing her key resources that will not conflict with her schedules. Whatever the solution, the key point is that you need to gain access to the go-to people and (1) inform them of your intention and (2) obtain buy-in from them so that you can get their support for your project. You will be surprised how willing people are to work with you if you do your homework and understand their agendas.

Assume that everyone in a political climate works on the basis of "what's in it for me." Incorporating this assumption into your business case will make it much easier to win over the critical go-to people and result in an easier path for getting your project approved at the top. The key is that you are able to articulate the "what's in it for them" and leverage the influence the go-to people have with the critical approvers at the executive level.

Influencer #2: Selection Criteria

Beyond the politics, the key variable for getting a project approved is meeting the selection criteria that have been established by your company or project approval committee. Sometimes these criteria are formally spelled out; other times they are ambiguous and not well known or understood. In either case, for a project to be approved it will need to pass a number of criteria by the authorities at large. Most criteria are based on fact and logic, but of course there may always be the case of a project being approved or not approved "just because."

Having a project approved or not approved "just because" falls in the category of politics and hidden agendas that we discussed in the Influencer #1 section. In any event, I do not want to spend time talking about the "just because" selection criterion due to the fact that it is ambiguous and not based on facts and logic that can be navigated for getting your project approved. What I do want to discuss are the selection criteria that are most common in organizations today and that, if met, will help ensure that your project will be approved for implementation. These criteria, which will be discussed in detail, are:

2-1. Project costs

2-2. Financial return

2-3. Strategic fit

2-4. Project risk

2-5. Soft benefits

2-6. Schedule

2-7. Resources

2-8. Location

Selection Criterion 2-1: Project Costs

The first selection criterion for your project are typically the project costs. Because many times project approvers state up front, "Great idea, but what is it going to cost me?" this is an area you need to focus on in order to provide sound justification. The best way to define your project costs is to first identify the project cost categories. Project cost categories are buckets of dollars where the project costs will be incurred. For example, cost categories can be software licenses, travel and expenses, training, building materials, labor, or external consulting, to name a few. Cost categories are not meant to be detailed accounting codes as found in a cash flow statement, but rather a grouping of major categories where the costs will be coming from. Be sure to identify all of the categories that you think will incur costs during the entire project life cycle.

After the cost categories have been defined, the next step is to determine the estimated cost for each of the categories (see Figure 1-9). To determine the cost estimates, you may need to obtain quotes from vendors and internal accountants as well as perform a rough analysis yourself. Each cost category should show the estimated costs to be incurred in each time period throughout the project life cycle. This time period can

FIGURE 1-9. Project cost estimates.

From the specified cost categories, project cost estimates should be determined for the financial project life.

Illustration

Cost Categories	2005	2006	2007	2008	2009	2010	Total Cost
Hardware	$1,000,000	$500,000	$500,000	$500,000			$2,500,000
Software License	$50,000	$50,000	$50,000	$50,000			$200,000
Travel & Expenses	$20,000	$20,000	$20,000	$20,000			$80,000
Training	$200,000	$200,000	$200,000	$100,000	$100,000	$100,000	$900,000
Internal Resources	$300,000						$300,000
External Resources	$300,000						$300,000
							$4,280,000

Project Cost Assumptions:

Describe details of the cost estimates including any assumptions for achieving the cost estimates.

Example: Assumes 2 servers required for volume of data; 200 user licenses annually for 4 years; internal and external resources required for project implementation in year 1 only.

be in years if your project is long term, or months, or even weeks. Be sure to include time periods beyond the project implementation if costs will be recurring after the project has been implemented, as would be the case with software maintenance or estimated sales commissions.

Once the estimates have been determined, any assumption about the costs should also be documented. For instance, you may be assuming that you will require 100 hours of outside consulting support, or that the number of software users will be thirty, or that travel will only include three trips to Philadelphia. Again, it is important to document any assumptions that you have relative to your cost estimates so that they can be reviewed and validated by the project approvers. By fully documenting the estimated costs and assumptions, you will then be able to provide a total cost estimate for the entire project. The total cost estimate can then be used to determine the financial return for your project.

Selection Criterion 2-2: Financial Return

Perhaps the most popular criterion for approving a project is the financial return. This is perhaps the one area that most executives pay the most attention. It is also the area that most people think of when they define a business case. Financial return can be measured in many different ways, however, the most important element is to show how much return you get for the money you invest in a given project.

Determining the financial return follows a similar process for determining the cost estimates. The first step is to define the financial return categories. These return categories should be any area that estimated savings or business impacts are to be booked. The financial return can be either cost savings (see Figure 1-10) or increases in efficiency or sales revenue. Examples are savings from reductions of billing errors, reduction in customer complaints, and inventory, or increased revenue due to higher product sales or greater market penetration.

Similar to the cost estimates, the financial return should be estimated in time periods. The time periods should be the same as in the cost estimates, so if the time periods are monthly in the cost estimates they

FIGURE 1-10. Financial return.

From the specified financial impact categories, savings estimates should be determined for the financial project life.

Financial Impact Categories	2005	2006	2007	2008	2009	2010	2011	Total Savings
Inventory Savings	$500,000	$2,300,000	$2,300,000	$2,300,000	$2,300,000	$2,300,000	$2,300,000	$14,300,000
Distribution & Logistics	$100,000	$300,000	$400,000	$400,000	$400,000	$400,000	$400,000	$2,400,000
Customer Complaint Reduction	$30,000	$40,000	$60,000	$60,000	$120,000	$120,000	$120,000	$550,000
Reduced Billing Errors	$30,000	$40,000	$40,000	$60,000	$80,000	$80,000	$80,000	$410,000
								$17,660,000

ROI: 96%   IRR: 40.3%

Discounted Payback (yrs): 3.1   NPV: $2.7 million

Financial Return Assumptions:

Describe details to the financial return estimates including any assumptions required for the savings estimates to be achieved. **Example:** Assumes annual inventory savings of $2.3M in year 2; customer complaint savings to increase annually based on increased call volume; billing error savings to increase annually based on increased invoices sent per year.

should also be monthly in the financial return. Once the financial return is determined for each category, the financial assumptions should be documented, such as reducing customer complaints based on a call volume of 1,500 calls per month, or reducing billing errors in proportion of the total amount of invoices per year. Documentation of the assumptions will again provide a means of validation by project approvers.

After you have determined the savings or revenue increases for the project life and have defined the project costs, you are then ready to begin calculating the benchmark metrics for financial return. The typical measures for financial return include:

Return on Investment, or ROI (see Figure 1-11)

Net Present Value, or NPV (see Figure 1-12)

Payback Period (see Figure 1-13)

Internal Rate of Return, or IRR (see Figure 1-14)

All of these measures show the return you get on your money based on the cost of the project versus the return on your investment. However, many of the financial return metrics offer pros and cons of presenting how good the return on your investment really is.

For instance, ROI, which is the most common measurement because of its simplicity, shows the magnitude of an investment based on a profit/cost analysis. Basically, this means that the higher the ROI number, the better the investment or financial return. But is this really the case? The down side to ROI is that even though the ROI number may be high, it may not always be better. For example, which is better, a 124 percent ROI on a $10,000 investment or a 60 percent ROI on a $300,000 investment? Without much thought you may say, "Of course, it's the investment with a 124 percent ROI." But if you do the math, 124 percent return from a $10,000 investment is only $12,400. On the other hand, a 60 percent return from a $300,000 investment is $180,000. Which would you rather have, $180,000 or $12,400? In this case the investment with

(text continues on page 40)

FIGURE 1-11. Financial return: return on investment (ROI).

■ ROI (Return on Investment):

- ROI is the most popular and most simple measurement to determine the financial return from an initiative that incurs cost.

- It can be calculated several ways within an industry. As such, it is not always the best measurement.

- It does not show magnitude of investment (e.g., which is better: 124% ROI on a $10,000 project or 60% ROI on a $300,000 project?).

Example calculation:

- ROI = (savings – cost)/cost x 100. **This is simple profit / cost analysis.**
- ROI = NPV of savings/initial investment x 100. **More precise with cash flows.**

FIGURE 1-12. Financial return: net present value (NPV).

■ NPV (Net Present Value):

– NPV is the present value of an investment's future net cash flows minus the initial investment. Generally, if the NPV of an investment is positive, the investment should be made.

– It takes into account discount rates.

– It is a standard financial calculation that does not vary within industry.

Example calculation:

$$NPV = \frac{CF1}{(1+r)^1} + \frac{CF2}{(1+r)^2} + \frac{CF3}{(1+r)^3} + \frac{CFn}{(1+r)^n}$$

CF = The net cash flow for each year that the NPV is to be applied

r = The discount rate or investment yield rate

n = The total number of years for which the NPV calculation is to be applied

FIGURE 1-13. Financial return: payback period.

■ Payback Period:

- The payback period is the length of time required to recover an initial investment through cash flows generated from the investment. It is simply the amount of time taken to break even on an investment.

- The payback period provides some visibility as to the level of profitability of the investment in relation to time.

- The shorter the time period, the better the investment opportunity.

- It is a standard financial calculation that does not vary within industry.

Example Calculation:

$$\text{Payback Period} = \frac{\text{Initial Investment}}{(\text{NPV of Savings} / \text{Years}_n)}$$

n = The total number of years for which the NPV calculation is to be applied

FIGURE 1-14. Financial return: internal rate of return (IRR).

IRR (Internal Rate of Return):

- IRR is the rate at which the present value of a series of investments is equal to the present value of the returns on those investments. Often called Average Annual Total Return.

- The IRR represents the inherent discount rate or investment yield rate produced by the project.

- It takes into account money earned by the investment (interest, dividends, capital gains distributions).

- IRR is similar to the NPV calculation with the exception that the equation is solved for the variable **r**.

Example Calculation:

$$\text{Initial Investment} = \frac{CF1}{(1+r)^1} + \frac{CF2}{(1+r)^2} + \frac{CF3}{(1+r)^3} + \frac{CFn}{(1+r)^n}$$

CF = The net cash flow for each year that the IRR is to be applied

r = The internal rate of return

n = The total number of years for which the IRR calculation is to be applied the lower ROI may be a better option. This is the downside of the ROI measure, which is why you may need to look at other financial return measures.

Another measure is the payback period for your investment. Simply put, the payback period is the length of time needed to recover your initial investment, which is another way of saying, the length of time to break even on an investment. The payback period provides some visibility as to the level of profitability of the investment in relation to time. The shorter the time period, the better the investment opportunity. This type of measure is pretty standard in industry and provides a solid perspective of when an investment will provide a return.

Both of these measures, used in conjunction, are perhaps the most common financial return measures used in industry. You can see, however, that one used without the other may not provide the best view for determining the financial return.

In addition, financial return as the only selection criterion may also not be the best way to determine whether a project should be approved. Remember our discussion on project business value and the benefits the project can bring to the business? Looking beyond financial measures is hard for many executives; however, it may be the difference when assessing the ability of a project to be successful or not. Consideration to how a project fits into the overall company strategy, project risk, required investment, soft benefits, timeline for implementation, and location are all other considerations to be taken into account.

Selection Criterion 2-3: Strategic Fit

Strategic fit for your project is quite simply the alignment of your project goals to the overall goals of the company. For instance, say the overall company strategy is to manufacture low-cost products for customers that are environmentally friendly. On the other hand, let's say that the goal of your project is to reduce costs of products by introducing new materials that are not environmentally friendly. The result is that the strategy of your project does not match the strategy of your company. Although your project will be producing low-cost products, it will be doing it in a way that does not fit with the company strategy. In this case, the strategic fit for your project is low. This may have an overall effect on your project being approved, especially in comparison to other projects that may be more strategically aligned.

Some companies perform a detailed strategic fit analysis using a weighting system for your project goals. This is especially the case with companies that focus on the research and development of products. The lesson here is that while putting together your project proposal, you as project manager should look beyond the tactical end of the execution and look at your project from the perspective of strategy. Ask yourself whether your project is strategically aligned with the company's strategy. If it is, you will have a much better chance of getting your project approved.

Selection Criterion 2-4: Project Risk

Project risk is an area within the business case that helps build credibility for getting project approval. Risk provides a foundation for leveling the perception of risk among management and the project team. What may be risky to you may not be risky to another person. By performing a risk assessment based on facts and not feelings helps establish a common platform for determining the true risk of a project and therefore enhances the overall probability of success. From a logical standpoint, if something has a low probability of success or involves very high risk, people tend not to want to engage in that activity. Having a common way to assess risk is then key to really understanding where your project sits in regards to the overall risk to the organization or the probability of achieving success.

Going through the exercise of a risk assessment also serves as a foundation for developing a *risk mitigation plan*. This type of plan puts in place actions that can be taken to help avoid the risk identified for the project. Having a plan to mitigate risk is, in many cases, just as or more important than knowing what the risk is overall. Again, a risk mitigation plan is another one of the elements that helps establish credibility, thoroughness, and demonstrates that you are prepared to ensure that your project will be successful. The result of assessing risk is that you now have a basis for reporting on risk throughout the duration of the project implementation. It also creates a basis for comparing your project to others within a project portfolio, so that one project can be compared to another in terms of its probability of success or risk to the business.

Risk, therefore, becomes another basis for comparison other than cost. For instance, what if your project costs more than another but has a higher probability of success? If the less expensive project has a low probability of success, perhaps it is not worth the time and effort to implement. Risk gives approvers a new dimension to help predict which project will be successful. Along with other factors, such as the soft benefits or schedule, it helps get beyond the "black and white" cost and begins to focus the organization on choosing the project that has the capability to deliver the most value to the organization—more specifically, to focus on which project has the highest probability that project value will be achieved.

To begin the risk assessment process, let's talk about the concepts of risk factors and risk ratings. *Risk factors* are used to identify the types of risk associated with a given project. There are three types of risk that can occur with a project:

1. Delivery risk
2. Business risk
3. Technical risk

Delivery risk is associated with ensuring a successful implementation of the project. For example, the success of your project may be at risk if you exceed you project budget, miss your project timelines, or deliver more project scope causing overrun of timelines and budget. Delivery risk is focused on the tactical side of the project implementation and can be any risk that would impede your ability to implement or deploy your solution to meet your project objective.

The second type of project risk is called *business risk*. Business risk is simply any risk that your project may pose to the overall business. One example of a business risk may be the ability to effectively transfer knowledge to the stakeholders. Without effectively transferring new skills, such as the ability to analyze new types of information as a result of your project implementation, stakeholders may not be able to perform their job effectively. This is a risk to the business. This risk also includes the ability to transfer information across cultures and languages—an issue particularly related to global projects.

Another example of business risk is the ability for the business to participate in the project. Say your project is being implemented during a high peak in your business cycle, such as at the end of a quarter or during key holidays. Conflict with other activities may result in low involvement of key business people, causing less buy-in to your project. Less buy-in leads to low stakeholder satisfaction, creating barriers for key stakeholders when you ask them to adapt to the changes required by your project. We will discuss more about this topic when we talk about stakeholder management.

The last type of risk is called *technical risk*. Technical risk is related to a specific technology or capability that your project will require as part of its implementation. An easy example may be the implementation of a new software application. If, for instance, the software is a new version or is introducing a new type of functionality, this would certainly be a technical risk in terms of the software working properly when it is needed for deployment. Technical risk, however, does not have to be linked to software. It can also be related to new equipment, tools, or the ability to acquire a building permit or even to meet certain legal or regulatory requirements.

Regulatory compliance, for example, is very common in health care companies and hospitals. For example, launching a new pharmaceutical product requires many iterations of testing and trials before a drug is approved by the Food and Drug Administration (FDA) for release to the market. This brings a certain technical risk to the project that can have a significant impact on the overall success. The same goes for acquiring a building permit. Risk is occurred whenever a new design or a change to a design is required. Obtaining the required permits is indeed necessary for the success of your project.

All of these examples fall under the technical risk category and should be identified as risk factors that can be used for developing an overall risk assessment for your project. Once all risk factors have been identified, the next step is to begin the overall assessment of project risk. To do this, you need to first weigh the importance of each risk factor relative to each other (see Figure 1-15). Based on a rating of 1 to 5 with 5 being the highest, each risk factor that you identified should be given a *risk weight*. As shown in the example in Figure 1-15, being out of scope (4) has a higher impact on project success than being over budget (3) or missing a scheduled date (3). Furthermore, not having the system function properly (5) is judged to have a higher impact on project success than all other risk factors.

After you have determined the importance of each risk factor, assign the appropriate weight percentage to each risk factor. To determine the weight percentage, first calculate the sum of all of the risk importance ratings (32 in Figure 1-15). Next, divide each risk factor importance rating by the sum of all the ratings. This is the weighting of the risk factor. For example, the weight for the scope risk factor is 13 (4 divided by 32, rounded up). Please keep in mind that the sum of all the weightings should total 100 percent.

When the risk factors have been weighted, the second step is to rate the impact that the risk factor may have on project success as well as the probability that each impact will actually occur (see Figure 1-16). The *impact rating* should be made based on a 1 to 3 rating. A rating of 3 means that the risk factor will have the highest impact on project success and will have significant cost and time implications to the project. A rating of 2 means that there is some impact on project success, but that risk can

FIGURE 1-15. Risk factors: importance weighting.

The first step in assessing risk is to weigh the importance of each risk relative to each other.

Importance

Delivery Risk	Rating 1 to 5 (5 highest)	Wt %
Cost	3	9
Schedule	3	9
Scope	4	13
Delivery Resources	2	6

Business Risk		
Business Participation	3	9
Knowledge Transfer	3	9
User Satisfaction	4	13

Technical Risk		
Technical Complexity	3	9
System Reliability	2	6
System Functionality	5	16
	32	**100**

% weight of each risk factor based on sum of ratings

Total weight must = 100%

Sum of ratings

FIGURE 1-16. Risk factors: impact and probability rating.

The second step in assessing risk is to rate the impact the risk factor has on project success and the probability that each impact will actually occur.

Risk Impact Definition:

1= Low; project success not significantly impacted (effect of risk can be contained)

2= Moderate; project success impacted somewhat (risk can be contained if appropriate measures are taken)

3= High; project success heavily impacted (risk has significant cost and time implication)

Probability Rating Definition:

1= Very unlikely to be manifested in this project

2= Likely not to happen in this project

3= Very likely to happen in this project

	Impact	Probability
	Rating 1 to 3 (3 highest)	Rating 1 to 3 (3 highest)
Delivery Risk		
Cost	2	2
Schedule	2	2
Scope	3	2
Delivery Resources	2	2

Business Risk		
Business Participation	2	2
Knowledge Transfer	2	2
User Satisfaction	3	2

Technical Risk		
Technical Complexity	2	2
System Reliability	3	2
System Functionality	2	2

be contained if appropriate measures are taken. A risk rating of 1 means that the risk is low and that the impact on project success is not significant and can be contained.

Once you have rated each risk factor according to its impact, the next step is to rate the risk factor according to the probability that it will actually occur. The *probability rating* is made on a scale of 1 to 3. A rating of 3 means that the probability of the risk factor actually occurring is very high. A probability rating of 2 means that the risk factor is likely to happen, and a probability rating of 1 means that the risk factor is very unlikely to manifest itself on this project. Gathering the input from other stakeholders as well as your knowledge of the project and business are good benchmarks for making your assessment. The idea is to provide a realistic and objective view so that the overall risk ratings will be credible.

After you have determined the risk factor weight and the impact and probability ratings, calculate an overall risk rating for the project (see Figure 1-17). Basically this is done through a *weighted average calculation*. To calculate the total rating for each risk factor, multiply the weight by the impact and probability rating. In Figure 1-17, for example, the risk factor for "scope" has a weight of 13, an impact rating of 3, and a probability rating of 2. As a result, the total rating for the scope risk factor is 78 (13 × 3 × 2 = 78). The sum of all total risk factor ratings equals the overall risk rating for the project. In Figure 1-17, the overall project risk rating is 457.

Using the overall risk rating matrix shown at the bottom of Figure 1-17, you can determine the overall risk of your project. For example, the overall project risk rating of 457 is considered a high project risk. This means that there is a very heavy impact on project success if risks are not mitigated. The overall ratings within the matrix go from Very Low to Low to Moderate to High to Very High. Obviously, the higher the project risk rating, the more that has to be taken into account for approving a project. In other words, a project with a very high–risk rating will have to demonstrate significant business benefits in order to justify approval. A high-risk rating means that there could be a significant im-

FIGURE 1-17. Risk factors: overall rating calculation.

The third step in assessing risk is to calculate the overall risk rating for the project by using a weighted average calculation.

Delivery Risk	Importance Rating 1 to 5 (5 highest)	Wt %	Impact Rating 1 to 3 (3 highest)	Probability Rating 1 to 3 (3 highest)	Total
Cost	3	9	2	2	36
Schedule	3	9	2	2	36
Scope	4	13	3	2	78
Delivery Resources	2	6	2	2	24

Business Risk					
Business Participation	3	9	2	2	36
Knowledge Transfer	3	9	2	2	36
User Satisfaction	4	13	3	2	75

Technical Risk					
Technical Complexity	3	9	2	2	36
System Reliability	2	6	3	2	36
System Functionality	5	16	2	2	64
	32	100			

Overall Rating   457

Overall Risk Rating Matrix

500+   = Very high project risk (project success will be heavily impacted and very likely to happen if risks not mitigated)
400 to 499 = High project risk (project success can be heavily impacted and likely to happen if risks not mitigated)
300 to 399 = Moderate project risk (project success impacted somewhat but not likely to happen)
200 to 299 = Low project risk (project success not significantly impacted and not likely to happen)
100 to 199 = Very low project risk (project success not significantly impacted and probability for failure is low)

pact on the business, and nobody wants that. Therefore the benefits will need to outweigh the risks in order for the project to ultimately be approved. One of the ways to overcome or at least help to justify a project with a high-risk rating is to develop a risk mitigation plan (see Figure 1-18). This is a great addition to any business case. The *risk mitigation plan* is a way to document a plan for mitigating each risk identified for your project. A plan basically consists of the action steps that need to be taken to avoid a particular risk. For instance, to mitigate being late on your project schedule, you might plan to engage in weekly status meetings with key stakeholders who are assigned tasks. In addition, you might make visible project schedules and weekly status reports to the project sponsors to whom the key stakeholders report. That way if there is a conflict, you as the project manager will be able to engage the sponsor to help address the issues and keep the project on time. These actions taken by you as project manager will help mitigate risk.

Within the risk mitigation plan you should also document who will be responsible for carrying out these actions. In some cases this may be you as project manager, or the action may be assigned to someone who will be required either to participate in the mitigation action or to be responsible for the mitigation action itself. The higher the total risk rating that you determined, the more detailed should be the actions you plan to help mitigate the risk. In the end, a good risk mitigation plan consists of realistic action plans, as well as people and time frames assigned for achieving those actions.

Selection Criterion 2-5: Soft Benefits

Approvers expect to see what "soft" benefits will derive from your project other than the hard financial numbers, if the project is successful. Soft benefits are intangibles that are difficult to measure or put a financial value on, such as customer satisfaction, employee morale, visibility of information, federal or regulatory compliance, brand recognition, or being environmentally friendly by making customers feel good about buying your product.

FIGURE 1-18. Risk mitigation.

Risk Mitigation Plan Report

Project: 77784368 - Supply Chain Optimization

Risk Type	Risk Factor	Risk Rating	Mitigation Plan	Responsible Owner
Business	User Satisfaction	○	Will involve all stakeholders in design workshops.	Project Manager
Business	Knowledge Transfer	●	To conduct stakeholder surveys throughout project life cycle.	Change Manager
Business	Business Participation	●	To conduct stakeholder surveys throughout project life cycle.	Project Manager
Business	Performance Measure	○	To establish & assign metrics to stakeholders prior to go-live.	Process Specialist
Delivery	Scope	○	Will involve all stakeholders in design workshops.	Project Manager
Delivery	Cost	●	Controller is part of project team.	Finance Team Member
Delivery	Schedule	●	Weekly review of project plan with updates to project sponsors.	Project Manager
Delivery	Delivery Resources	○	Vacation planning to be approved by managers ahead of time.	Project Manager
Technical	System Functionality	○	Conduct 3 cycles of testing.	Test Lead
Technical	Technical Complexity	○	Include detailed integration testing with legacy systems.	Test Lead

The importance of discussing soft benefits is that they establish further justification for "why" your project needs to be approved. Sometimes the reason your project needs to be approved is simple, such as the business needing to comply with certain regulations. Other times it is because there is a greater good beyond the financial returns—or even in addition to the financial returns. The soft benefits are important because they help tip the scale in getting your project approved. This helps get beyond the "black and white" financials and helps establish the broader perspective for success: the project value to the business.

Selection Criterion 2-6: Schedule

The sixth selection criterion is the project implementation schedule. Executives always want to know when a project will be implemented. Many ask "how fast." The *project deployment schedule* is a way to concisely present the deployment plan (see Figure 1-19). Although you may have prepared a very detailed analysis or schedule, it is not necessary to present every activity of your project plan. The project approvers will just want to know the key project milestones. A *milestone* is a major event or activity that will occur as part of your project execution. From PMI's *PMBOK®* (*Project Management Book of Knowledge*) or a standard project execution methodology, these major milestones include Initiate, Plan, Execute, Monitor, Close. Once you as project manager have determined the major project milestones, the start date and finish date should be documented as part of the business case.

In addition, you should also document any implementation plan assumptions. In doing so, this will highlight any particulars that need consideration as part of your project implementation schedule. For example, let's say that your project will be launched at the same time as the major industry trade shows. Because during this time business tends to dip, the immediate benefits from your project implementation may be delayed. There are many planning assumptions that should be thought about while putting together your project deployment schedule. The idea is to fully document them as part of your business case.

FIGURE 1-19. Deployment schedule.

The deployment schedule shows the key milestones for the project implementation life cycle.

Key Milestones	Planned Start	Planned Finish
Initiate	4/2/2007	6/1/2007
Plan	6/2/2007	8/1/2007
Execute	8/10/2007	11/1/2007
Monitor	11/2/2007	12/15/2007
Close	12/15/2007	12/31/2007

Implementation Plan & Assumptions:

Describe details of the deployment plan including any assumptions required for the plan to be achieved. **Example:** Launch of new systems to be coordinated with November trade show; test systems to be available during execution and testing stage of project.

Selection Criterion 2-7: Resources

The seventh selection criterion is resources. Without resources your project will not get done. Competing for resources is always a major business constraint, along with competing for budgets. From the resource standpoint, this section of the business case is to focus more on the types of resources that you need rather than the individual names of the people (see Figure 1-20). Types of resources include project managers, technical specialists, accountants, legal representatives, sales, and other department or functional areas. Along with the types of resources that will be required to implement your project you should also identify whether the resource is internal to your company or an external resource like a customer, contractor, or consultant.

Once the type of resource has been identified, the next step is to estimate the number of hours that they will be required to participate on the project. This is typically documented in monthly or weekly buckets in an effort to get a holistic picture of the requirements. The goal is to determine the total number of hours that these resource types will be required, after which an estimated cost can be calculated by multiplying the total hours by a standard rate for that resource type. The standard rates can be determined simply by taking an average rate for each resource type. Your company accountant or controller can provide you with this standard rate. Be aware that you may have a different rate for an external resource type (typically higher) even if that same resource type exists internally within your company.

The sum of the total costs for each resource type will provide you with the grand total estimated resource cost for the project. This is the number that many executives will focus on while reviewing your business case. After the total resource cost has been estimated, you should then document any assumptions about the resources in order to provide a complete picture of your resource needs.

For example, you may assume that no vacations will be taken during November because this is a critical time for your project, or that a specific resource like the controller will be available to participate on your project

FIGURE 1-20. Resource estimates.

For the business case, the project roles are more important than the individual names required for the implementation. As such, the type of resources and estimated hours will determine the estimated resource cost for the project.

Total hours × standard rate for internal and external roles

Project Role	Type	Apr	May	Jun	Jul	Aug	Sep	Oct	Nov	Dec	Total Hrs	Total Cost
Project Manager	External	120	160	160	160	160	160	160	160	160	1400	$210,000
Tech. Lead	Internal	80	80	120	120	120	120	120	120	120	1000	$65,000
Team Leader	Internal	120	160	160	160	160	160	160	160	160	1400	$91,000
Process Specialist	External	40	40	40	40	40	40	40	40	40	360	$54,000
Controller	Internal	10		10		10		10		40		$2,600
												$422,600

Resource Assumptions:

Describe details to the resource plan including any assumptions required for the plan to be achieved. **Example:** No vacation for project resources during November; controller to be available for 10 hours every other month.

at least ten hours every other month. Whatever the assumptions, it is better to document them than to assume something that may not come to fruition. Approval of your business case means approval and/or validation of your assumptions. If for some reason your assumptions are not approved, then you will at least know that you need to make other plans and can adjust your business case.

Selection Criterion 2-8: Location

The project location is the final selection criterion to be considered. The project location is defined by where the project implementation is actually going to occur. The reason why this is important is that the project location may have an impact on resources, facilities, culture, language, and business conditions. For instance, a project to be located or implemented in Mexico may be good from the perspective of cheaper labor costs, but there may be issues regarding the resources required to implement the project. For instance, if many of the project resources with the required skills are located in the corporate office, it means that travel arrangements (including visas and passports) and expenses need to be taken into account.

Having the project located outside of the United States may also present cultural and language barriers that may ultimately increase the overall risk of the project. Or, say that the facility where you are proposing to implement your project has just gone through a major change or will be going through one at the time you are proposing to deploy your project. These are all types of issues that you need to think through ahead of time so that you will not get blindsided when your project business case is up for review.

Influencer #3: Leadership

Although your business case may satisfy the political angles and all of the selection criteria, *leadership* could be the one influencer that derails your ability to get your project approved. Time and time again I have seen projects fail because of the lack of leadership. What do I mean by leader-ship? I believe leadership of a project occurs at two levels: (1) the actual project leader who runs the day-to-day operations, and (2) the executive sponsors of the project who oversee the execution of objectives and help clear the path for achieving them. Without both levels of leadership, the project is destined to fail.

Based on many industry surveys as well as my own experience over the last twenty years in running projects and advising clients at Fortune 500 companies, the result is always the same. Without executive buy-in through the duration of the project as well as effective leadership on the day-to-day basis, projects will almost always fail to achieve their original objectives. This is because leadership drives the strategic vision for a proj-ect as well as the execution of the project. Forget politics, forget selection criteria. While these are both important barriers to overcome in getting your project approved, without effective leadership project success will not be achieved.

Leadership is where the "rubber meets the road" in implementing the results and it is the key variable to an executive feeling "warm and fuzzy" when providing final approval. What do I mean by "warm and fuzzy"? This is the "gut" feeling that an executive has when asking, "Do I think this leadership team will not only complete this project, but get the job done by achieving all of the project's objectives?" It's as simple as that.

If an executive can confidently answer this question "yes," there is no doubt your project will be approved. Why? Because good executives know that the mere completion of a project does not mean that objec-tives will be achieved. They know that the day-to-day operations need to run effectively as well as be supported by key executives to ensure that road blocks are being removed and that the project will succeed. Just like a CEO has a board of directors, a project leader needs an executive sponsorship team. Together this leadership team will handle the execu-tion of the project to achieve results or project objectives even if com-pleted on time and on budget.

Having said all that, I do want to underscore the fact that the project leader is the key variable in the leadership team. Without the day-to-day activities being run smoothly and issues being identified and addressed properly, the project may fail, even when a good executive sponsorship team is in place. As such, a proven project leader remains the ultimate determinant that gives executive approvers their "warm and fuzzy." I think of it this way: If I had to have an operation, would it be okay if my surgeon completed the operation on time and budget but failed to achieve the desired result? For me, it would not be acceptable if I had to go through all the pain of a surgery and yet I was not confident that the surgeon was able to achieve the objectives of the surgery. I would no doubt make sure that this surgeon knew what he was doing and had a track record of getting the job done, even beyond my own personal "warm and fuzzy."

Although this is a drastic example (and I hope the proposed project is not as life threatening), the thought process is the same. The leaders of a project have to portray that same confidence level to the executive approver. Can they get the job done by driving the strategic vision and achieving the overall objectives? Like selecting a surgeon and the surgical team, selecting proper leadership is critical to the overall success of a project. It is similar to a CEO running a company with the approval of the board of directors. If the board is not confident that the CEO will achieve results, what happens? That's right, the CEO will not last very long in that job. Selecting the proper project leader and leadership team is critical to the success of getting your project approved.

Influencer #4: Business Case Presentation

The final sign-off for your project may come, not because of all the details, but because of how well you can articulate all of the key aspects of your business case. This is where what matters is not only a solid presentation of the facts, but more importantly, a presentation of facts that can be understood. A business case should be thought of as a sales presentation of facts, figures, and a plan for getting the job done in terms of achieving all of the objectives. Like anything in life, if you cannot simply and concisely communicate the who, what, when, where, why, and how, the project may just be passed over, even though it may be the best thing since "sliced bread." A business case should be well documented, but not to the degree of a book or dissertation. It should have enough detail, but not too much detail that the overall picture may get overlooked or, even worse, not be understood because it is too confusing.

Think for a second of a meeting you have attended recently where you spent an hour listening to issues, details, and discussions, and where you walked out of the meeting saying, "What was that all about?" That is NOT what you want to have happen when you present your business case. You want the opposite to happen. You want the attendees (the executives approving your project) to walk out of the meeting saying, "I get it . . . this is good . . . when can we start!" To have this happen, it all comes down to presentation and the ability to articulate your vision for success.

So what do I mean when I say presentation? A presentation comes in three forms:

1. Pictures
2. Paper
3. Pitch

Pictures can be the way that establishes the vision of what your objectives are and how you are trying to achieve them. They can range from a formal Microsoft PowerPoint presentation where your ideas are described in bullet form along with diagrams, to informal illustrations that you draw during the presentation. Pictures are a great way to ensure that your points are well understood, since most people are visual. Anything that can make your idea for a project well understood in a concise fashion will help in getting your project approved. Executives don't have a lot of time to spend analyzing your business case; they would prefer to just see the bottom line and details in summary form.

Paper is another important way of communicating your business case. This can be the physical representation of facts and figures in a Microsoft Word document, Microsoft PowerPoint, or spreadsheet format; something that executives can take away and read later, if they want. Typically, approvers who are heads of finance departments or CIOs are the ones who want to see the details and do the comparisons to other similar projects. Even chief executives will want to know that you have spent the time on the details, although some may not want to read them. As such, it is important not to get too bogged down in the "paper" form of the business case, but provide enough information to accommodate the standard polices and procedures within your company.

How much is too much? I would say that an effective business case can be documented in ten pages or less. Anything more is too much detail. If you follow a proven method of exactly what type of information should be provided, then this can easily be accomplished. Remember the purpose of the "paper" idea is to back up the presentation that you are making about your business case with enough detail and analysis to make your points valid and credible. Without this, no approver will take your proposal seriously.

Pitch is of course the verbal presentation to the appropriate approvers, whether this is one person like your immediate boss or an assembly of the proper approvers. The pitch is what ties the pictures and the paper part of the presentation together and will bring it home to getting it approved. In some cases your pitch may need to be consolidated into a minute or less if you are meeting one on one with an executive and need to get to the point fast, perhaps even during a ride in the elevator.

This is sometimes called an *elevator pitch*. This means that you must be able to get to the main drivers of what you are trying to do and most importantly the b .... s. That's right, the benefits (I hope you were not thinking of something else). The benefits are all about the value that the project will bring to the organization. If you only have 30 seconds to pitch your project proposal in an elevator, I am sure that the executive you are speaking with will not want to hear about your getting the project done on time and on budget, but rather want to know what is in it for the organization in terms of benefits and project value. This will be the basis for further discussion and interest for an executive to want to hear more.

On the other hand, if you are not pitching your project to an executive in an elevator, but rather in a meeting to a handful of the designated project approvers, you will want to pitch something different right? Wrong. During a more formalized meeting you should take the same consideration into account and get to the point quickly in order to grab their interest in hearing "how" your plan will be achieved. The pitch is just as it sounds; it is a sales call for your project. Get to the point fast, clearly and grab their attention. Get them interested in hearing more.

This means that you must be prepared with the paper analysis, the pictures that will articulate the vision and road map for driving the benefits, and the pitch for verbally communicating the key points and getting them excited for approving your project. All three are important and all three will be the key to getting your project approved. The result will be for all attendees to leave the meeting by saying, "I get it . . . this is good . . . when can we start!"

SEVEN PRINCIPLES FOR DEVELOPING A WINNING BUSINESS CASE

With all this said, over the years I have developed what I call the seven key principles for developing a winning business case (see Figure 1-21):

1. *Obtain advanced buy-in from steering committee members and key managers who have approval authority.* As we discussed, the leadership team is a key variable to getting your project approved. Meeting with them before your project is actually pitched is one way to ensure that when everyone is sitting around the table looking at each other and saying, "Should we do it?" they will nod their heads "Yes." Test your project proposal pitch ahead of time with your project approvers. This will help clear up any

FIGURE 1-21. Developing a winning business case: Seven principles.

1. Obtain advanced buy-in from steering committee members and key managers who have approval authority.

2. Be able to demonstrate "how" the business benefits will be achieved with a sound probability of success.

3. Gain commitment and support from the "key influencers" in the stakeholder community.

4. Set realistic expectations.

5. Develop a feasible implementation plan.

6. Articulate "why" your project fits within the overall budget and "why" the timing is critical to the business.

7. Keep the presentation simple and easy to understand.

misconceptions as well as gain the appropriate support before any formal meeting is held. If you think this is "politicking," it is, and it could be a differentiator in getting that final Yes.

2. *Demonstrate "how" the business benefits will be achieved with a sound probability of success.* Discussing "what" you are trying to do without demonstrating "how" it can actually be achieved will do little to help your cause. Executives want to know that what they will be investing in from the standpoint of money, resources, and time will have a high probability of success. Demonstrating "how" your project will achieve benefits or project value is the ticket to getting your project approved.

3. *Gain commitment and support from the "key influencers" in the stakeholder community.* This tackles the politics of working the key influencers that you identify early in the process. Answering the question of "what's in it for them?" will be the key for avoiding political roadblocks. You will need the buy-in from the key influencers in order to gain buy-in from the top. Access to stakeholders is sometimes easier than getting access to the top executives who are needed for the ultimate approval. If navigated properly, a smooth buy-in process can be achieved.

4. *Set realistic expectations.* Nothing can be worse for your career than selling your approvers a "bill of goods," just to get your project approved.

In order for you to be successful as a project leader in the long run, you must set realistic expectations. Make sure that what you say you are going to achieve is actually achievable. This means being realistic with time-lines, benefits, utilization of resources, issues, etc. Being honest up front will gain you not only credibility but establish your reputation for saying what you are going to do and doing what you actually said. Having this reputation is what will move you up the ladder in your career.

5. *Develop a feasible implementation plan.* A feasible implementation plan is critical for establishing the feasibility of your overall project pro-posal. Since the implementation plan will use critical resources as well as time and energy from the organization, executives are keen to see a real-istic timeline based on their own logic. If you as a project leader fall short in this regard and present something that is not feasible, your proposal will get the axe. Don't cut yourself short on time and don't overestimate the timeline so that you will come in ahead of schedule. Provide a plan that will allow your project enough time to achieve the benefits. Being realistic about when project benefits will be achieved is the best policy and will enable you to deliver against a roadmap that executives can benchmark to measure the results.

6. *Articulate "why" your project fits within the overall budget and "why" the timing is critical to the business.* As important as "how" benefits will be achieved is "why" benefits need to be achieved. Discussing why a project needs to be implemented and why it must be implemented *now* creates a sense of urgency in terms of competition, government or legal regula-tion, and business climate, among others. These are all key variables that weigh in when the approvers make their final decision. You don't want your project to be put on hold for later implementation. Do your home-work and align your project with the sense of urgency needed to get it approved.

7. *Keep the presentation simple and easy to understand.* As discussed be-fore, the presentation is the sales pitch for your project proposal and may

be what puts it over the top for approval. Although you will need to work on the details, your presentation must be simple and easy to understand. Executives need to talk about your project and sell it up the chain of command, and if they "get it" in terms of their understanding and logic, there will be no doubt that it will make the top of the list for getting approved.

Following these seven key principles as a rule of thumb during the entire business case development process will surely be a way of getting your project approved.

STEP 4: PROJECT SELECTION TECHNIQUES

Getting your project approved comes down to not only navigating the business case influencers and supporters but also how your project is viewed compared to others along the selection criteria previously discussed. The bottom line is project risk versus reward. In Figure 1-22, a typical risk reward chart is used to help with this comparison among projects. Many forms are used within the industry to compare risk and reward among projects, however the most common is the "bubble chart" since each project in the chart is represented by a bubble.

In this example, the size of the bubble represents the overall cost of the project. Along the "y" axis is the net present value (NPV), and on the "x" axis is the probability of project success. The probability of project success is calculated from the overall project risk. Using this bubble chart, an approver would want to choose a project that has the highest NPV, highest probability of success, and the lowest overall project cost. In the example in Figure 1-22, the financial reporting project may be the best fit for this selection criterion. It has the highest NPV, a low cost, and a probability of success that is about 57 percent. By balancing all of these factors, this project may bring the highest reward relative to the cost with a good chance of it successfully meeting its objectives. Other projects may be selected over this one based on the actual criteria used

FIGURE 1-22. Risk and reward chart.

The *"bubble chart," provides a comparison of projects for selection. Many forms are used within the industry, but all compare some sort of Risk and Reward for project comparison.*

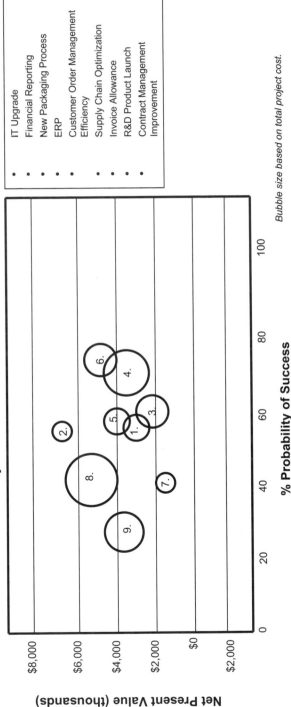

Project Risk & Reward Chart

Legend:
- IT Upgrade
- Financial Reporting
- New Packaging Process
- ERP
- Customer Order Management Efficiency
- Supply Chain Optimization
- Invoice Allowance
- R&D Product Launch
- Contract Management Improvement

Bubble size based on total project cost.

% Probability of Success

Net Present Value (thousands)

by the selection committee, but the financial reporting project makes good sense as well.

A comparison among projects is made along with the overall considerations as documented in the business case. Many criteria are used and many business case influencers are factored in for selecting a project for approval. The fact still remains, however, that the project that provides the best and fastest return on its investment with the lowest risk to the business will win almost every time; this, coupled with realistic cost estimates, a feasible implementation plan, and the best strategic and tactical blend for achieving the project business objectives.

STEP 5: THE BUSINESS CASE APPROVAL PROCESS

Until now, we have spent a lot of time discussing the approval process, but not actually how your project gets formally approved. The formal project approval process varies by organization and project types. Formal project approval is important because it ensures accountability for budget spending, for time and resource allocation, and it provides a reference for establishing a project performance tracking process. Actual project approval comes in several different forms.

The most basic form is obtaining a *verbal approval* for your project. Typically, verbal project approvals are used for small or fast projects, or in organizations that are less formal or small in size and have a streamlined bureaucracy.

A *formal signature* for approving a project is probably the most common method for approving a project, and it is a typical method within larger companies. Generally this method involves several different approvers, ranging from department heads, directors, VPs, to even CEOs— depending on the size of the budget and project. Formal signature approval may be electronic via workflow capability within a software technology or a manual signature on the business case document itself.

Sometimes formal signature approval for a project may be required for the initial start of the project as well as during each major project stage. This may be the case for longer duration projects, like ERP or R&D projects. Regardless of the form of the project approval, the best practice is to monitor the ongoing project performance and risk and reward. This ongoing monitoring will help determine whether the project should continue during its project life cycle or whether it should be put on hold or cancelled during the various life cycle stages.

As we all know, things change during the project execution. As such, it is important that the project value is always held in question and that it be assessed periodically to see whether the objectives are being met on a continuous basis. The business case, therefore, should be recognized as not only a document that outlines a proposal for obtaining funding and resources, but an action plan for achieving business benefits by realizing project value.

The following Project Business Case Exercises in Appendix A relate to the topics discussed in this chapter:

Exercise A-1: Project Initiation Document

Exercise A-2: Initial Assessment

Exercise A-3: Risk Assessment

Exercise A-4: Resource Requirements

Exercise A-5: Total Project Cost

Exercise A-6: Financial Return

CHAPTER 2

EXECUTING A PROJECT WITH A BUSINESS VALUE MINDSET

Once the business case has been successfully presented and approved, the next step that we have learned as project managers is to begin the project execution. We have learned that good project management is all about execution. We were all told that good execution is all about tactically managing our resources, scope, timelines, quality, and budget. But as discussed in Chapter 1, project success is not just about the tactical execution of being on time and on budget.

A successful project is about delivering project business value to the company. To deliver overall project business value we must look beyond the tactical execution of a project and focus on the strategic achievement of project value. This is the missing link. We as project managers have been so focused on the tactical end of executing a project that we have been missing the strategic link for getting our project from the business case to the actual achievement of the project business benefits.

At my workshops and seminars conducted throughout the country, I often ask how many project managers actually go back after implementing their project and measure the results as stated in the original business case. In this quick survey I often get a minority saying that they actually go back or are asked to go back and measure the results. Most respond by stating that they are asked to move on to the next project and never look back. This always amazes me in that all this time and effort is spent on putting a business case together and getting it approved, but at the end of the day nobody checks or measures the results.

How can this be? By focusing on only the tactical side of project execution we miss the whole point of why we are implementing the project in the first place. Many executives or project managers may not want to know the results of the project, mostly because they suspect that if they actually measured the results they would be disappointed. This is counterintuitive in that these are the very same questions that are asked during the business case process about how you will deliver the value to the business. The projects that are successful are the very projects whose success is measured.

To measure success means that you must have benchmarks in place and a mechanism for capturing the results. It also means that the execution of the project is based on the end game you have in mind. This is done by having an expectation of achievement as well as implementing a process that is geared toward delivering the results. Companies that have this mindset are the same companies that have as part of their project culture a focus on delivering business value in terms of reduced costs, business growth, speed, and efficiency, as well as the ability to maintain operations. These are the companies that we always hear about in terms of being the most profitable and of being successful benchmarks for getting the job done right. Getting the job done means delivering project business value. With this said, it is the project manager with this same strategic focus who is always the one getting promoted and considered the "go-to" person for getting the job done.

Delivering project business value starts with the execution of a project with a strategic focus, not just a tactical focus. It means that as project manager, you need to put effort up front during the planning stages to determine "how" your project will deliver project value. This is done through changing the future in terms of the vision for operating in a new way; realigning behaviors of the people in terms of making them accountable for results; and delivering the benefits by putting in place a long-term process for measuring and tracking the project results. To put this long-term process in place, project value must be planned and executed as activities within your overall project plan. This means that during the planning stages of your project, you as project manager must begin to think about the original business case and "how" your project will actually lay the foundation for project business value.

Typically this is done by imbedding key steps throughout the project implementation plan, which are geared toward achieving project value. For instance, within the project initiation stage there should be specific steps related to stakeholder management, communication planning, and risk management. These steps should include introducing stakeholder management as a concept to the leadership team. You should then conduct the first part of stakeholder management, which is identifying who they are and assessing them in order to establish how they will be managed throughout the duration of the project.

The same applies to communication planning and risk management. Communication planning steps include developing a project communication strategy and determining communication methods and responsibilities for managing stakeholder communication within the organization. Risk management includes identifying project risk factors, rating those factors, and putting a risk mitigation plan in place. Stakeholder management, communication planning, and risk management are critical foundation enablers for delivering project value. These foundation enablers along with the other steps (like KPI development and organizational alignment) are all part of the Project *Speed2Value*™ Road Map and should each have a process that is imbedded as part of the overall project plan. By including them as part of the overall project plan, they will not be overlooked as the project gets executed.

Putting the thought up front about each of these *Speed2Value* activities begins to establish the link between the strategic and tactical execution of a project. This is where the dots become connected and where you as project manager are forced to think in terms of delivering project value and not just in terms of tactical project execution. The process steps involved in the Project *Speed2Value*™ Road Map activities are topics that we will discuss throughout the remaining chapters of the book.

DEFINING PROJECT VALUE DRIVERS

The best way to execute a project plan with a project value mindset is to start by defining project value drivers. This is the second step in the Project *Speed2Value*™ Road Map (see Figure 2-1).

Project Value Drivers are best defined as a road map that articulates the various drivers that link the project business case objectives to accountability within the organization. I call this the Project Value Driver Map (see Figure 2-2). This map shows "how" your project will actually deliver the key business objective you stated in the original business case which was approved.

In the example of a Value Driver map shown in Figure 2-2, the key objective is reducing cost annually by $2.3 million. The map shows how $2.3 million in savings will be achieved for a supply chain reengineering project. The first part of the map shows which performance and financial drivers will be used for this project. Both the performance drivers and the financial drivers come directly from a typical balance sheet. The performance drivers in this case are revenue growth, operating margins, and capital efficiency. For this example of a supply chain project, all three performance drivers will be utilized. Other projects may only use one or a combination of performance drivers. The point is that in order to show how the business objective will be achieved, performance drivers will always come into play.

The financial drivers in this example, supply chain project, are volume, sales and general administration (SG&A), and inventory. All are standard balance sheet financial elements, and in this case all are critical for reducing overall costs (our main project value objective). The other financial drivers for this example do not come into play but may be

FIGURE 2-1. The Project *Speed2Value*™ Road Map: Value Drivers are best defined as a road map that articulates the various drivers that link the project business case objectives to accountability within the organization.

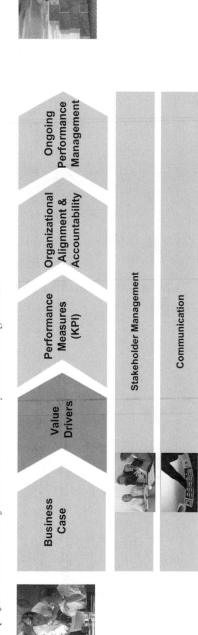

FIGURE 2-2. Sample value driver map linking the business objectives to accountability within the organization.

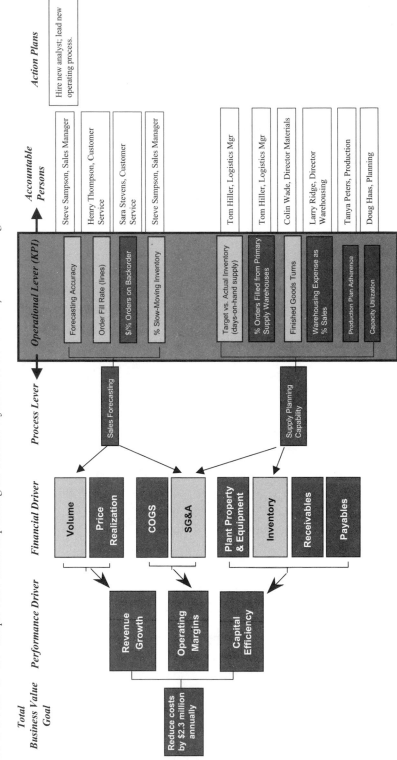

required for other projects. What the Value Driver map shows in this case is that this supply chain project is going to reduce costs by driving down inventory and SG&A expenses and improve the accuracy of sales forecasting by increasing sales volume and getting product to the right place at the right time.

Although you may not be able to see this directly from the map, a supply chain project typically hits these financial drivers in order to achieve success—in this case, reduced costs. As you put a value driver map together for your project you will need to go through the same thought process for the value drivers and levers.

Once you have determined the performance and financial drivers, the next aspect of the value driver map is to specify which process levers will be required to enable the balance sheet flow in order to meet your project objectives. In the case of this supply chain project, the process levers are sales forecasting and supply planning capability. Both of these process areas may be affected by changes in procedures and calculations, or by the introduction of new systems for determining sales forecasts or product supply plans.

The key point is that these will be the process areas that the supply chain project will focus on to drive the project objective of reducing overall costs. For any given project the process levers can be any process that requires change. That process could be order management, procurement, construction, loan processing, or any process that is particular to your organization and is a key lever for driving your project objective.

KEY PERFORMANCE INDICATORS

Now that you have defined the process levers, the next step is to determine the operational levers. Operational levers are the *Key Performance Indicators* (KPIs) that are required to drive your process change toward achieving your project objective. KPIs are defined as a measurable variable that is related to a series of process steps whose performance can be managed and delivered against a particular corporate or project objective.

In the case of our supply chain project example, there are four KPIs identified. These are:

1. Sales forecast accuracy
2. Order fill rates
3. Dollar amount of orders on back order
4. Slow moving inventory

Each of these KPIs are operational level measurements that serve as the key enablers for driving the process change and helping achieve the overall objective of reducing costs within the supply chain. For the supply planning capability we have identified an additional six KPIs that will act as drivers for reducing costs in the supply planning capability process. KPIs are all operational in nature because any given process is operational. We will discuss the development of KPIs a little later in the chapter, but for now understand that KPIs are critical enablers for driving a result. Without them we do not have a measure of success that can be managed on an ongoing basis. More importantly, because KPIs are operational, we can link them to people within the organization (stakeholders) who will be accountable for them on an ongoing basis.

Assigning Accountability for KPIs

Assigning KPIs to particular people in the organization is really the bottom line to this whole value-driver process. Having a project objective is one thing. Having accountability for making that objective happen is the area where most projects fail. We spend so much time talking about how great our project is in terms of the objectives it is going to achieve, but very little time putting in place the accountability process for ensuring that it will actually happen. Being specific about who is responsible for a particular KPI is a very bold but required step if you really want to drive results.

I am sure you have heard the phrase, "You manage what you measure." This phrase holds true here as well. If you identify the proper KPIs and assign accountability for them within the organization, most likely they will be managed appropriately and show results. Better yet, if these assigned KPIs all have action plans, along with specific steps for achieving them, the results will surely come.

The purpose of the Project Value Driver map is to do just what it states: Drive project value to achieve a desired strategic result. In the case of the supply chain project that we have been using as an example, the strategic result is to reduce overall costs within the supply chain. With the Project Value Driver map you can see "how" the $2.3 million in cost reduction will actually happen. By looking at the map, you can see which company performance and financial drivers will be involved, which processes you will be focusing on, which key performance metrics you will use to track your progress, and, most importantly, "who" is accountable and "what" action plans are going to be put in place to make all of this happen.

By having this Project Value Driver map, you are no longer rolling the dice, hoping that the project objectives will be achieved. You now have an actionable plan that is not only visual, but easy to articulate to all levels within the organization. The nice thing about the map is that it forces you, as project manager, to view your project not only as a tactical execution, but as a strategic execution for achieving results. This is a great way to close the gap of that missing link between tactical execution and strategic achievement that we have all had over the years.

Expressing KPIs

Let's go back to the discussion about Key Performance Indicators (KPIs). As we discussed, KPIs are critical operational performance measures related to a process that can be used to manage the results you set out to achieve on your project. KPI development is the third step in our Project *Speed2Value*™ Road Map (see Figure 2-3).

KPIs can be expressed in different ways, including cost, time, quality, service, or volume (see Figure 2-4):

(text continues on page 78)

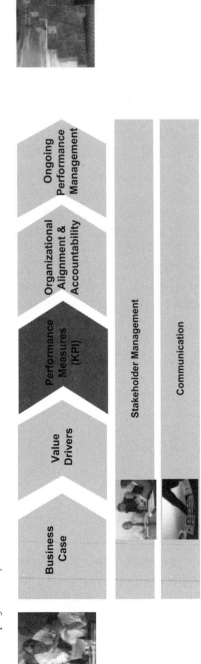

FIGURE 2-3. The Project *Speed2Value*™ Road Map: Performance measures. Key Performance Indicators (KPIs) are used to manage the results of the project that you set out to achieve.

FIGURE 2-4. Key Performance Indicators can be expressed in different ways.

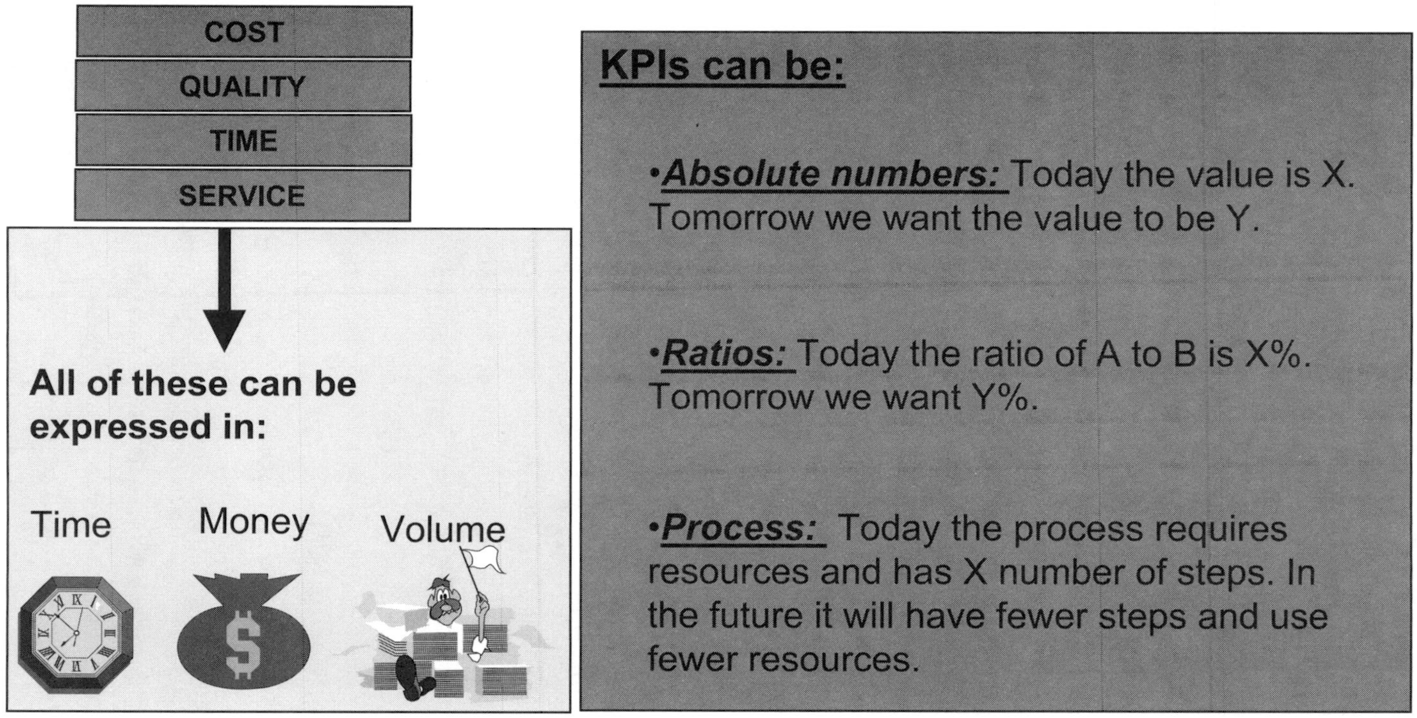

KPIs can be:

• **_Absolute numbers:_** Today the value is X. Tomorrow we want the value to be Y.

• **_Ratios:_** Today the ratio of A to B is X%. Tomorrow we want Y%.

• **_Process:_** Today the process requires resources and has X number of steps. In the future it will have fewer steps and use fewer resources.

COST

QUALITY

TIME

SERVICE

All of these can be expressed in:

Time   Money   Volume

- *KPIs can be absolute numbers.* For example, the price of my Johnson & Johnson stock is $58 per share; in one year I want it to be $70 per share.

- *KPIs can also be expressed in ratios.* For example, today the occupancy rate of our apartment complex is 70 percent; in six months we want it to be 87 percent.

- *KPIs can also be expressed as a process step.* For example, today our order management process—from taking a call to fulfilling the order—takes 27 steps and involves seven different people to service a customer. In three months we want the process to be streamlined and take only five steps involving just three people.

Each of these examples shows how KPIs can be used to help drive some sort of result. In the example of reducing the number of order management process steps, the result will be to reduce the cost of performing that process, not only in time, but in the number of people needed to perform the work. In the case of the stock price, the KPI is linked to driving more dollars or value. In the case of the occupancy rate, the KPI is linked to volume. All are operational in nature, and all will need to involve some sort of process or change improvement to be achieved. It doesn't really matter what the form of the KPI is as long as it is expressed in a way that can be clearly understood and that it is measurable.

Developing KPIs

To develop a KPI will take some thought from you as a project leader, as well as involve input from others within the organization. There are several considerations in developing KPIs. One such consideration is first determining what you need to measure. By looking at the overall project objective and the process or change that it involves, you may see more clearly what you need to measure. For example, if you are looking to grow your business by increasing sales, there may be several variables that contribute to driving sales volumes. One might be the number of sales people you have. Another might be the territory in which the product is sold. Or another may be the product type that is sold. To deal with these variables, several KPIs can be put in place to measure the progress of sales and help drive the end result of increasing sales overall within your company.

For instance, one such KPI may be to measure sales dollars by territory. This may help determine from which part of the country most of the sales are coming or in which part to the country sales are lacking. Perhaps the Midwest has the highest sales by territory and the Southeast has the lowest. By having the sales-by-territory KPI in place, you will then be able to measure progress and put plans in place to help generate sales in the deficient territories. Another KPI may be to measure sales by salesperson. This will help determine which salespersons are productive and which ones are not. By knowing this you may be able to identify best practices from the higher performers and share them with the lower performers in an effort to increase sales overall.

Measuring sales by person may also help determine whether more salespeople are required in your organization by looking at the maximum sales by person over time. This may help identify that if increased sales is the project objective and the maximum sales per person is X dollars, then additional sales people will be required to drive more sales overall. In looking at both the sales-by-territory and the sales-by-person KPIs together, you may be able to identify where the new salesperson should be located, whether in the territory with the lowest sales volume, or in a newly created territory.

Determining what KPIs you should use for your project takes strategic thought. There may be many KPIs that can be used to drive the same result. In Figure 2-5, we see that improving customer service has many such KPIs. In this example, the KPIs that could be used are the number of products delivered on time, the quality of delivery, the number of

FIGURE 2-5. Key considerations: the components of service.

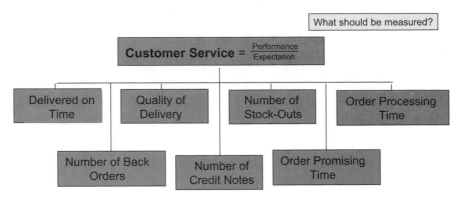

stock-outs, the time it takes to process an order, just to name a few. All of these KPIs are good measures and all would help improve customer service.

How many KPIs are enough and which are the best ones to use? Best practices are to keep the number of KPIs down to a manageable level, say seven or ten at the maximum. Any more than that, I have found, an organization gets into "analysis paralysis." This means that any more than ten well-defined KPIs will move the organization into spending more time on gathering and analyzing the information for a KPI metric than actually managing the process that the metric is supposed to help drive.

I know of a leading industrial manufacturer that had over 45 KPIs to measure supply chain performance. Each KPI was processed as part of a report distributed to over a dozen managers. I learned that only three of the managers even looked at the reports and even then they did not know the definitions of all but a few of the KPIs, and even worse, did not understand their implication. Not only were the KPIs not being looked at, they also differed from one manufacturing facility to another. Nobody was responsible for them. When I spoke with managers who had looked at the KPIs, they shrugged their shoulders and stated that there was no way that the KPIs could be achieved. I won't even go into the cost of generating and distributing the information for the KPIs.

The point is that most KPIs are meaningless unless they are clearly visible and simple enough to understand. Too many KPIs are just noise to the organization unless they have direct links to individual or group performance that is understood, visible, and rewarded if achieved. To help keep KPIs visible they should be cascaded throughout the organization from top to bottom. Those who are measured by them need to know that others are looking at them as well and are using them to make judgments about individual and team performance. KPIs should be realistic so that they can be viewed as attainable by those who have to achieve them. They should be linked to rewards and incentives and included as part of the overall compensation program so that they can change behavior. If people know how their performance is to be judged they will more than likely work toward making sure that they manage their daily activities to include the KPIs.

To this point, KPIs should be reported in a timely manner so that performance can be corrected if needed. In addition, KPIs should be standardized across the organization so that all KPIs are calculated the same way to avoid discrepancy and keep the focus consistent across the different parts of the organization. Lastly, KPIs should be part of an ongoing performance management process so that they can be enforced and managed long after the project has been completed.

For the industrial manufacturer with 45 KPIs, none of these best practices were engaged, at least not until we put a project together to make it so. At the end of the day, we were able to get the manufacturer back in line, cutting back from 45 to managing 7 KPIs, all linked to compensation and aligned with the overall supply chain cost-reduction project. The net result was an overall manufacturing cost reduction of 75 percent in the first year. This was accomplished by following the best practices for KPI development just discussed.

Measuring KPIs

Now that you have seen how to determine what KPIs you should use for your project, the next thing to consider is how to actually measure them. Sometimes the same KPIs can be calculated in different ways. In

order to ensure that KPIs are understood and bought into by the stakeholders they must agree with how the KPI calculation is actually made.
For instance, in Figure 2-6 you can see the same KPI calculated in three
different ways. In this example the KPI is delivery reliability used in the
manufacturing of a product.

In the first example, delivery reliability is calculated by dividing the
total number of production orders that are produced with the correct
time and quantity by the total number of production orders that are produced overall. By using 3 correct production orders out of 10 produced,
the delivery reliability is 30 percent.

A second example to calculate delivery reliability is to use the quantity of total actual production divided by the total planned production.
This is a KPI calculated by looking at the production quantity only. By
using an example of 1,040 actual units produced divided by 1,000 units
planned to be produced, we get delivery reliability of 104 percent.

The third way to determine delivery reliability is to calculate the KPI
from a financial viewpoint. In this example, delivery reliability is calculated by dividing the total actual dollars produced by the total planned
dollars to be produced. Using an example of $16,000 actual production

FIGURE 2-6.   Key considerations: sample KPI calculations.

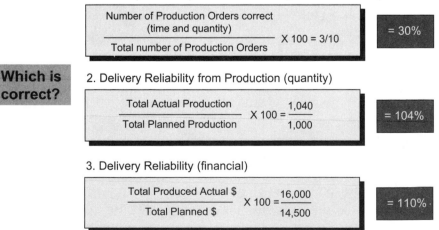

1. Delivery Reliability from Production (production orders)

$$\frac{\text{Number of Production Orders correct (time and quantity)}}{\text{Total number of Production Orders}} \times 100 = 3/10 \qquad = 30\%$$

Which is correct?

2. Delivery Reliability from Production (quantity)

$$\frac{\text{Total Actual Production}}{\text{Total Planned Production}} \times 100 = \frac{1,040}{1,000} \qquad = 104\%$$

3. Delivery Reliability (financial)

$$\frac{\text{Total Produced Actual \$}}{\text{Total Planned \$}} \times 100 = \frac{16,000}{14,500} \qquad = 110\%$$

and dividing it by $14,500 planned production, we get delivery reliability of 110 percent. None of these examples are wrong, but all of them tell a slightly different story.

Getting Input for the Use of KPIs

The bottom line is that there are not only many different KPIs that you can use, but many different ways that KPIs can be calculated. The lesson in all of this is that if people or stakeholders are to be measured by KPIs, they should play an active role in helping determine not only what KPIs should be used but also how they should be calculated. Without active input by a senior or respected member of the group or the actual stake-holder that will be measured by the KPI, all will be lost when you try to implement the project. With this said, getting input while developing a KPI is critical. Aside from getting input from the people within the organization, several other kinds of input can be used for developing a KPI (see Figure 2-7).

Input from the Business Case

One such input is the original business case. The business case is often overlooked after the project has been approved. The business case, how-

FIGURE 2-7. Inputs to KPI development.

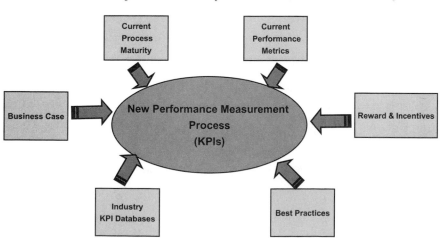

ever, is a critical document that should be referred to while implementing your project. As we discussed in Chapter 1, one of the key elements within the business case is the documentation of the business benefits to be achieved. These details were put into the business case not just to provide the justification for getting the project approved but to lay the foundation for delivering the project benefits to the company.

It is your job as project manager to review the business case as part of your project planning in order to identify which areas were designated for driving the benefits. Coupled with the Project Value Driver map, these process areas are the point at which you should start your development of the project KPIs. As such, the business case is a critical input to your development of a KPI.

Input from Existing KPIs

Another such input are current KPIs or metrics that are being used in your organization (or at least being gathered, as in the case of the industrial manufacturer previously discussed). A great way to use existing KPIs is to start by determining how effective they are. More times than not the link between the current KPIs and the process that the project is focusing on is a great indication that something is not working. The reason for your project is to improve or implement some kind of change.

An existing KPI is obviously not being used properly if your project has been approved to change something in the current process area or operation that the KPI is related to. Problems with the existing KPI can be related to several things. It just may not be visible to the people who are accountable for it. Or it may be calculated in a way that the people who are asked to manage it don't accept and therefore do not buy into. Or it may just be inappropriate for the operation and not show the true impact or picture related to operational performance. Whatever the reason, the use of existing KPIs is another great starting point in your development of a new performance reporting structure. In some cases the current KPIs will work just fine, and in other cases they will need either to be reworked, standardized, or replaced with new, appropriate ones.

Input from Process Maturity

Along with the existing KPIs, you should also look at the current *process maturity level*, by which I mean the ability for the existing or target process to adapt to managing the new performance metrics. Basically a very manual process with lack of technology and low integration to downstream processes will have a more difficult time delivering against advanced metrics.

For example, if you implement a KPI, such as order processing time in an order-management process that is very immature, your chances of seeing improvement in that measure will be slim. The reason is that the variables to order processing require a process that crosses many boundaries, including the sales department, the order fulfillment department, and the shipping department. To improve upon the order-processing KPI, all of the departments must have (1) visibility to the information once the sales order is placed, (2) systems that can track the flow of the order between departments, and (3) shipping data once the order has been completely processed. With a manual process, this KPI will have a difficult time yielding ongoing improvements. It can, however, be used as a means of determining a benchmark for improvement. The KPI for order processing is good if the project objective is to improve customer service as a whole by reengineering the process and implementing new integrated systems.

Input from Current Rewards Programs

Current rewards and incentives programs are another good input to developing KPIs. As we discussed, for KPIs to be effective they must be incorporated as part of an incentive program. Typically this includes bonuses or even softer incentives like vacation days or concert tickets. Looking at how current rewards and incentives drive performance is a great way to determine whether something is working or not. If performance is not to the level it needs to be to meet your project objectives, then you have good justification for making your new KPI part of a reward and incentive program. After all, if we can agree that people are the key driver for achieving project objectives, then linking your KPI to people and rewarding their achievement for meeting objectives is a no-brainer.

Input from Industry Standards

In case you do not know where to start developing a new KPI or eliminating existing KPIs, a good starting place is an industry KPI database. Much research has been done gathering industry benchmarks as well as metrics that have been used successfully. Today most industry KPI metrics come standard as part of leading software packages, such as SAP, Oracle, Business Objects, SAS, ValueCurve, and Primavera, to name a few. All of these software packages come with a good standard KPI database, and they also have the capability to manage the KPI usage across the organization. Industry-related organizations, such as the Supply Chain Council and other research-related consulting firms, also collect data to compile KPI metrics on the industries they serve.

Keep in mind, however, that metrics used elsewhere may not always be a good fit for your organization or project. Sometimes one size does fit all and other times it does not. Looking beneath the KPI calculations—who will be accountable for them and where they will be visible—are all considerations for implementing new or revising old KPI metrics. Remember that the KPIs that you develop need to work within your environment.

The most important thing about your organizational environment is that it has its own culture, history, and people associated with it. This makes it particular to your organization, which is a good thing, but it is also something that needs to be navigated in order to get the job done. Getting the job done means looking beyond the tactical project implementation and leading your project change strategically so that all of your project objectives can be met and measured with sound KPIs on an on-going basis.

Leading the change process is the subject of Chapter 3.

ACHIEVING PROJECT VALUE

THROUGH STAKEHOLDER

MANAGEMENT

Let's take a step back. We have so far discussed the first three steps of the Project *Speed2Value*™ Road Map. The first step was to develop the business case in an effort to obtain executive buy-in and set the stage for achieving project value (Chapter 1). The second step was to establish a project value driver map to help define "how" your project will deliver the project business value (Chapter 2). The third step was to determine your Key Performance Indicators (KPIs) for measuring the project results (also Chapter 2). Before moving further along the Project *Speed2Value*™ Road Map, it is now time to discuss the common thread that ties the original business case to the measurable benefits to be achieved. This common thread is called *stakeholder management*. Stakeholder management is one of two foundation enablers of the Project *Speed2Value*™ Road Map.

If we look at the overall objectives of any business, we can categorize them into four areas, all delivering value to the business. The first category is to *grow the business*. I don't know many executives who don't want to grow their business, whether it is market share, overall sales, brand awareness, or anything else that will make their business bigger, more powerful, and better leveraged in terms of size and capability. Having the ability to grow means that you are able to put to work more resources, whether it is people, financing, or facilities and equipment to cover more ground and penetrate a market in terms of sales. Growth for many companies is the key to long-term viability.

The second business objective category is to *become more profitable*. Even big companies with big sales may not be as profitable as they need to be in order to grow. After all, it is always about the bottom line. For a company to become more profitable means that it must reduce its costs. Cost reduction has been a main focus for companies since the industrial revolution. In fact, approximately 60 percent of a product or service is made up of the cost of materials or labor. In some cases it may be even more. The ability for a company to reduce costs relates not only to being more profitable, but to being able to price your products and services cheaper in the marketplace to be more competitive. There is no doubt that the existence of more players in the market today constantly drives down prices, while the cost of materials and labor in all industries—whether it be construction, manufacturing, professional services, financial, or healthcare—is on the rise. Your ability as an organization to reduce these costs is your key to being more competitive and more profitable. If you fail to do that, you will soon be out of business.

The third business objective category is to *operate with faster speed and greater efficiency*. With cost reduction as a major focus, employees today are having to make do with fewer resources. I am sure you have often said, "Don't worry, boss, I have plenty of people to help me out, plenty of time to do my job, and all the tools I need to do my job more effectively." Yeah, right. The fact is that in today's world we are all forced to do more with less. Less time and money, and fewer resources and tools. This means that if you want to go home at night and spend time with your family, you are forced to become more efficient. This is the same deal, in general, for companies. The ability to manufacture more products in a day, build more highways and housing faster, or service more customers better is all about having the people within the organization being able to work faster with fewer resources and produce more output. That is being more efficient.

The final business objective category is to *maintain operations*. Sometimes growth, cost reduction, or speed and efficiency are not the main focus for a business. It may just be a matter of complying with a legal regulation like the Sarbanes-Oxley Act, or obtaining permits required to build a house, or meeting FDA requirements to launch a new product. Or your objective may simply be to comply with company standards while putting in place a new process or technology required to keep things running within your organization. Maintaining operations is sometimes just as strategic as some of the other business objectives, and is considered to be a valuable goal for a business.

The bottom line is that whatever the business objectives may be, companies execute things called "projects" in order to meet them. Projects can be formal or informal, but are put together for the sole purpose of meeting a goal aligned with one of the four business objectives. The goal is intended to bring value to the business, whether it be growth, reduced costs, speed and efficiency, or maintaining operations. Delivering this value is what your project is all about.

To execute your project means that you will involve a combination of three things: processes, organization, or technology. Some projects may involve all three, and others just one or a combination of these areas. For example, if you are implementing a new tool or mechanism, you will be using technology, and most likely processes to ensure that the tool will be used properly by the people within the organization. If you are constructing a new house or facility, you will be using an organization (in this case subcontractors) to build it, you may use a process (perhaps new) to manage it, and you may or may not be using technology to facilitate the overall construction.

The fact is that whatever the project, it will most likely involve one or more of these three areas. All of these areas involve people. People follow a process. People are part of an organization. People use a technology. Therefore, if projects are used to achieve business objectives (growth, reduced costs, etc.) and projects fall into one of the three categories (processes, organization, technology), then people are the foundation of achieving business value. I think it is said best by George F. Colony, the CEO of Forrester, a leading technology research company:

> Deploying technology without changing process and organization will create little impact—and it often brings negative consequences. Naked technology wipes out productivity improvements, hurts return on investment, and dulls the bright edge of well-conceived strategies.

Changing the way people work (processes) or how they work together (organization) is critical to any project, whether it be implementing a new technology or constructing a new bridge. It takes people to make it come together and make it happen. And making it happen requires change.

CHANGE MANAGEMENT

The process of making change happen is a term we often hear, called *change management*. Although there are many definitions of change management, I define it simply as the process of moving from a current state to a desired state for the purpose of improving the business. Change management involves:

1. *Shaping the future* through business strategy
2. *Realigning behaviors* of the organization
3. *Delivering the benefits* to the business

Effective change management consists of active:

- Communication
- Stakeholder management (individuals or groups affected by and capable of influencing the change process)

- Project and business risk management
- Performance and reward
- Organizational alignment
- Skill competency
- Leadership

By looking at the top fifteen project issues based on a recent survey from PM tec, Inc. (see Figure 3-1), you can see that seven out of the fifteen issues, or 47 percent, are related to *change management* (indicated in bold in Figure 3-1). The top two issues are explicitly all about change management. These are:

1. Lack of executive support and leadership
2. Lack of change management and/or accountability for project results.

The rest of the seven change management issues highlighted in bold are:

3. Poor communication
4. Change to business requirements
5. No link to business objectives
6. Insufficient or inadequate business involvement
7. Team roles lacking clarity

Given the fact that people are involved in change and change is inevitable as part of any project, change management becomes probably one of the most important aspects for achieving project success. Looking across the typical causes of poor project performance (see Figure 3-2), you can see that elements of change management are scattered throughout each of the categories of poor performance. Whether it is project assimilation, project structure, building a business case, or having a process in place to maximize project business value, change management is an important element in helping achieve project success. Think for a moment of one of your recent projects. Was change management a critical factor in your project's success or failure?

(text continues on page 94)

FIGURE 3-1. Top project issues from PM tec, Inc., survey.

1. **Lack of executive support & leadership.**
2. **Lack of change management and/or accountability of project results.**
3. Insufficient or inadequate resources.
4. **Poor communications with business and/or team.**
5. Scope changes are not managed properly.
6. Competing business agendas.
7. Project schedules not realistic.
8. Roadblocks are not resolved in a timely manner.
9. **Changes to business requirements.**
10. **No link to business objectives.**
11. Too many projects competing for the same resources.
12. Budget overrun.
13. **Insufficient or inadequate business involvement.**
14. Project team isolated from the business.
15. **Team roles & responsibilities are unclear.**

Source: Project Performance Survey, PM tec, Inc.

FIGURE 3-2. Causes of poor project performance.

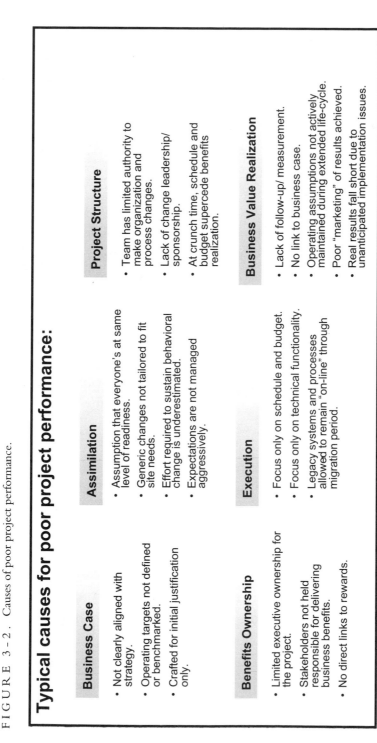

Typical causes for poor project performance:

Business Case

- Not clearly aligned with strategy.
- Operating targets not defined or benchmarked.
- Crafted for initial justification only.

Assimilation

- Assumption that everyone's at same level of readiness.
- Generic changes not tailored to fit site needs.
- Effort required to sustain behavioral change is underestimated.
- Expectations are not managed aggressively.

Project Structure

- Team has limited authority to make organization and process changes.
- Lack of change leadership/ sponsorship.
- At crunch time, schedule and budget supercede benefits realization.

Benefits Ownership

- Limited executive ownership for the project.
- Stakeholders not held responsible for delivering business benefits.
- No direct links to rewards.

Execution

- Focus only on schedule and budget.
- Focus only on technical functionality.
- Legacy systems and processes allowed to remain "on-line" through migration period.

Business Value Realization

- Lack of follow-up/ measurement.
- No link to business case.
- Operating assumptions not actively maintained during extended life-cycle.
- Poor "marketing" of results achieved.
- Real results fall short due to unanticipated implementation issues.

FIGURE 3-2. Causes of poor project performance.

There are many different types of change that a project can create. Change can come from new technologies, such as new application systems, new products, or new technical infrastructure (e.g., networks and e-mail systems). Change can come from new organizational boundaries, such as new or merged departments that involve new locations or geographies. Change can come from projects that have an impact on corporate culture, such as new bosses or leaders, new working environments, or working in new zones, which is a frequent issue in global projects and very relevant to companies that outsource operations. Finally, change can come from processes, such as new policies and procedures that must be followed or new skill sets that must be acquired to perform a job. Companies and people must navigate across these many types of changes as part of any project to achieve success. Not doing so means your project will fail. It will fail to be on time and on budget and, more importantly, fail to meet its intended objective of delivering project value to the business.

If you are like most people, you probably don't like change. Change takes effort, it takes focus, it takes being uncomfortable for a while until you get used to the new way of doing things. Whether you are following a new process, using a new tool or technology, or part of a new organizational structure, change is happening. People say all different things about change, like "I don't understand why we are doing this" or "This doesn't fit with the way we do things around here" or "I'm happy with the way things are, we're doing OK." Change happens and it is critical that you and your team become part of it. You know the saying, "the only thing that is constant is change."

Here's a quick exercise. Think for a moment about a recent project that you were involved in that required change. What was the change objective? What type of change did the project require? What went well? What didn't go well? How did people's behavior influence the change? What did you learn from the experience? Use the worksheet in Appendix B, Exercise B-1, "Your Experience with Change," and write down your answers.

After doing this exercise I am sure that you would agree that change is not an easy thing, not only for yourself but for other people. Managing change is a science and an art because it involves people, it involves emotions, and it involves focusing on the end goal of changing the behavior of people to reach a project and business objective. There is a direct link to achieving business value by managing change (see Figure 3-3).

I think of it this way: 80 percent of the effort for implementing a project is focused on implementing the solution. This is what I call "laying the foundation," or executing a project to meet on-time and on-budget objectives. At best, laying the foundation will only help achieve 30 percent of the business value that the project was approved for. The other 70 percent of the business value will come from having people accountable for the change that is to be implemented as well as following a value realization plan to ensure that the project value is actually achieved. Being accountable for change means that you have a clear plan in place that identifies what actions are required for the change and who is accountable for the results.

It also means that you have metrics in place that will help manage the change process, diagnose when and where problems arise of not being able to deliver the project benefits, as well as continually improve the process of being accountable for change and delivering project value or benefits. Realizing the overall project value gets down to being able to link the original business case to the stated value to be achieved, putting in place tangible and intangible metrics to measure the project value delivered, and identifying gaps in project value achievement so as to put corrective action plans in place to get back on track and keep focus on delivering results.

It is this last 70 percent of delivering the project business benefits where most projects fail to put the effort and fail to ensure that the benefits promised in the original business case are actually linked to the results achieved. Most companies only achieve, at best, the 30 percent of the benefits from implementing the solution. Executives then sit back and say, "How come we spent all this money and didn't get the benefits we thought?" This is

FIGURE 3-3 . Achieving business value by managing change.

Developing key performance measurements, holding people accountable for results and managing the change process are critical steps for realizing value.

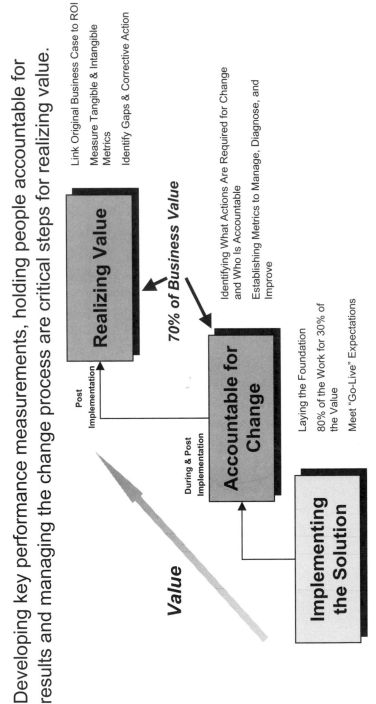

Realizing Value

Link Original Business Case to ROI

Measure Tangible & Intangible Metrics

Identify Gaps & Corrective Action

70% of Business Value

Accountable for Change

Identifying What Actions Are Required for Change and Who Is Accountable

Establishing Metrics to Manage, Diagnose, and Improve

Laying the Foundation

80% of the Work for 30% of the Value

Meet "Go-Live" Expectations

Post Implementation

During & Post Implementation

Implementing the Solution

Value

exactly the case when you look at some astounding statistics: 57 percent of SAP customers believe they have not achieved a positive return on investment, and failure rates (on time and on budget) for projects have been increasing over 18 percent for the last six years (Source: PMI survey).

Something is missing. Companies today are running more projects than ever, but at the same time achieving less business value from these projects than ever. If we can agree that project success is more than being on time and within budget and scope, and that it must also include satisfying the business need by being linked to an overall business strategy as well as be acceptable by business stakeholders and customers, then we can more clearly see the root cause of the problem. Two other success criteria involve change and stakeholder management. Without satisfying the business need and being accepted by stakeholders, the effort spent, even if the project is executed on time and on budget, is for nothing. This is a simple concept but somehow seems to be constantly overlooked, and it results in many projects failing to deliver to the expectations set out in the original business case. So what do we do about it? We need to get serious about stakeholder management.

STAKEHOLDER MANAGEMENT

Stakeholder management is the process for managing the people related to our project and inevitably being accountable for delivering the project results at the end of the day. Simply put, a *project stakeholder* is anyone who is affiliated with a project who can potentially have a positive or negative influence on the end results. Typical stakeholders include:

- *Individuals*: President, project sponsors, project managers, process owners, team members, system users, department managers, and supervisors

- *People in Groups*: Executive committee, steering committee, line management, specialists, and support staff

•   *External stakeholders*: Customers, suppliers, shareholders, government agencies, trade unions, and consultants

Stakeholders are important for many reasons. The main reason is that stakeholders provide buy-in and consensus to change. Without buy-in, stakeholders will become fearful of the change and begin to have negative reactions that will end up derailing the change effort. A project manager must realize that failure to lay the groundwork early in managing stakeholder reactions will create many problems downstream as the project progresses. To lay the groundwork early, you need to involve key stakeholders in the process even before the project gets started. For example, involve the financial or accounting department while you are establishing the project budget. This may avoid stakeholders questioning the budget or the need for additional funding, because the budget is supported by the credibility of an "approved" third party. Similarly, you can involve key stakeholders in developing the design change (whether a new process or technology) or the implementation plan. By letting stakeholders be part of the solution, it may eliminate them as part of the problem later on. Getting buy-in to any aspect of your project as early as possible is a great way to manage stakeholders and eliminate potential barriers and derailment during the project life cycle.

Project managers should also understand that not all stakeholders see change the same way, and they can have different reactions. I may see change as a great opportunity for me to showcase my newly acquired skills, where you may see it as a threat to your job and the way you have been doing things for the last fifteen years. To help in this effort; leading companies use a *cascading sponsorship* network that leverages executive buy-in and helps with getting authority figures behind the overall project change effort. The cascading process typically comes from top management down so that support of the project endeavor is firm and can be easily disseminated throughout the organization.

Almost like a mandate, but hopefully softer in terms of establishing a vision for change, a cascading network helps obtain buy-in throughout the ranks across the organization. Cascading sponsorship is one of the top project issues, and getting this buy-in at the top remains a critical success factor. Remember the business case justification that was approved? Keeping an ongoing relationship with the stakeholders who approved the original business case is the best way to build a cascading network.

Stakeholders react to change differently during the entire project life cycle (see Figure 3-4). When a project first starts, typically stakeholders will have high expectations. In most cases this means that they perceive that the project will succeed easily and will achieve not only your project objective but many other things as well. At least that is how the business case described it, right? Not really. As the project gets underway, the stakeholders then start to realize the level of effort that is required by them as well as the level of complexity. "They never said it was going to take this much time" or "Wow, this is more difficult than I thought" are typical comments that I have heard about a third of the way down the project life cycle.

The result of this realization by stakeholders is despair. Quite frankly, they get overwhelmed and they begin to panic. This is where projects begin to unravel. This is also the point where you as project manager begin to spend more time on the politics of the project, because the people in despair are starting to complain about your project, everything from time to budget and effort to objectives. At this point all the doubts about the project begin to surface, and others within the organization—including the bosses, the sponsors, and team members—now get involved. During the despair stage of a project, you as project manager spend less time executing and more time handling the issues, politics, and emotions of all the people involved. This is the part of the project that causes the most pain, and this is the stage of the project where most projects fail.

With a little luck and perseverance, you as project manager will hopefully navigate through the despair stage of the project so that those stakeholders, sponsors, and bosses in despair will begin to see the light at the end of the tunnel. Typically this happens about two thirds of the way through the project life cycle. That is when a sigh of relief is heard and

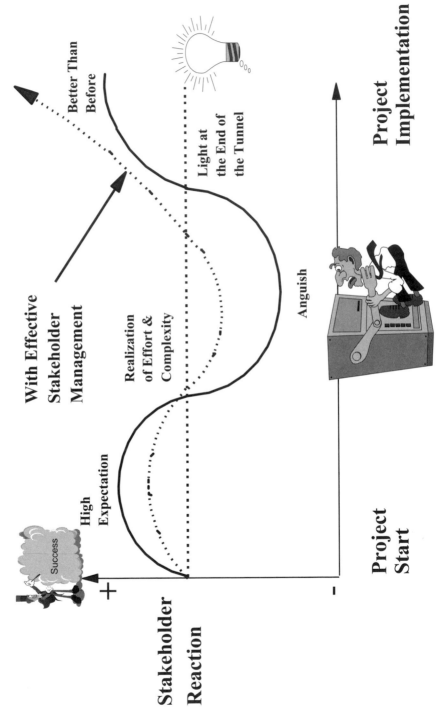

FIGURE 3-4. Stakeholders' reaction to change.

the light bulb clicks on in the stakeholders' heads. From this point on, stakeholders should begin to realize that the project that they have diligently been participating in is starting to provide some results, not only for the business, but more importantly, for them. This, then, is the point where they say, "Wow, this is better than it was before." Whatever the project, whoever the stakeholder, and however long the project life cycle, I would be surprised if either you as a stakeholder, or someone you managed as part of your team, has ever responded in a similar way at an earlier stage in the project. Think about that project involving change, which you identified earlier. Am I right?

With effective change management, we as project leaders can help stakeholders navigate through this response to the change process. We can help set more realistic expectations up front by communicating to our stakeholders that the project will take effort on their part and will not happen automatically. Identify up front where the areas of complexity and effort will come into play and what will be required for them. Keep reminding the stakeholders that the bumps are coming, so that they can be prepared before they arrive. Communicate to the project sponsors that the heavy lifting is coming and that some despair among stakeholders may surface. This will help address the politics early and keep emotions at bay so that you as project manager can keep control and let others know that you have command of the project from start to finish. Understand better the stakeholders' thought processes when they reach the point of despair and help them navigate through those difficult times.

We can encourage stakeholders by working with them to visualize success and help move them toward the light at the end of the tunnel faster. It is up to us as project leaders to manage change and not be engulfed by it for the sake of our stakeholders, our project, and our business. Hold on and help others to hold on, and remember that as the tide rises, all boats rise.

Another way to look at stakeholders' response to change is to follow and understand their thought processes (particularly during the point of despair) through the "zipper curve" (see Figure 3-5). It is called a zipper

FIGURE 3-5. Zipper curve: Stakeholders' commitment to change.

Commitment
"I am committed to this change."

Positive Perception
"I see the opportunity for me with this change."

Engagement
"I see how this project may impact me."

Understanding
"I know what you are talking about."

Awareness
"You are telling me something about this project."

Compliance
"I will do it if I have to."

Negative Perception
"I feel threatened by this change."

Obtaining commitment requires:

Communication
Leadership
Help from All Team Members

curve mainly because the picture looks like a zipper. The concept is not to have your stakeholders get caught in the zipper or the middle and to make a positive decision to be committed about the change that is taking place as a result of your project. Basically, this curve very nicely articulates the stakeholders' commitment to change as the project progresses.

Starting at the bottom, awareness is created when a project first starts. This may be the first meeting that the stakeholders attend and the first time that they are being told about the scope and objectives of the project. They typically just sit back at the awareness stage and quietly listen to all that you have to say. As the project progresses, they begin to understand what the project is about. They have attended more meetings or received many status reports and project documents, and they begin to absorb what the project is all about. Then they begin to get engaged in the project as they attend more meetings or are assigned work activities. During this time they begin to see what the implication is for them.

This is the turning point in the process, where stakeholders now intuitively make a decision about how to perceive the project. If not managed properly (e.g., by having attended a poorly managed project meeting or by being allowed to see the personal implication as threatening or the amount of work as overwhelming), they may have a negative perception of the project. This is the beginning of the point of despair, which we saw in the stakeholders' reaction curve (Figure 3-4). If this is the case, they will continue on the path of absorbing the change and reacting to it, and sometimes so negatively as to derail the project.

Through proper communication, leadership, and support from team members, however, stakeholders can be managed to have a positive perception of the change. As a result, they will support the project change effort and become a change advocate or leader. On the positive side, they will want to help achieve the change created by this project. On the negative side, they will go along just because they have to, which may lead to their becoming a barrier to the project as it progresses.

The key here is to follow a stakeholder management process that influences more project stakeholders to the right of the "zipper curve" than to the left. You must realize that not all stakeholders will move in the positive direction to the right, but the more the better. It is important not to have anyone stuck in the zipper and not be able to make a decision one way or the other. Knowing where they stand will help you better manage them as stakeholders and help the project move down the path of success. The bottom line is that without the commitment of stakeholders, change will not occur within the organization. As a result, new systems or processes will not be used, people will go back to the old way of doing things, and realization of results will not be achieved.

The key is to manage stakeholders by linking them to value drivers of the new systems or processes. This can be done by mapping them to performance targets, establishing accountability plans, developing incentive programs, and most importantly, developing a culture so that the change sticks.

STAKEHOLDER MANAGEMENT AS A PROCESS

To make the change stick, stakeholders can be managed through a proven approach. This is the stakeholder management process (see Figure 3-6). This is a three-stage process that identifies stakeholders, analyzes them, and then puts an action plan in place to manage them through the entire project life cycle and beyond so that the project objectives can be achieved.

Identify Stakeholders

The first stage in this process is to identify the stakeholders. Stakeholders are anyone who is affiliated with a project and who can potentially have a positive or negative influence on the project. Stakeholders should be identified regardless of whether they have been allocated to a project (made part of the project team). When identifying stakeholders, try to identify everyone, don't try to minimize the list. It only takes one person to set a project on the path for derailment. If all stakeholders are identified, you will have a better chance to put an action plan in place to

FIGURE 3-6. Stakeholder management process.

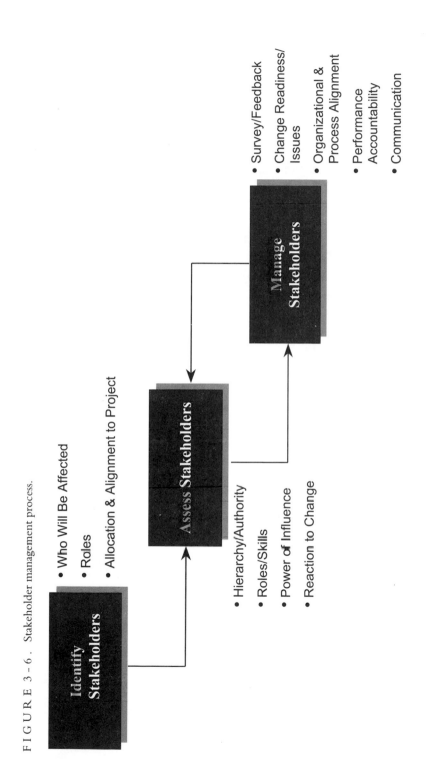

Identify Stakeholders

- Who Will Be Affected
- Roles
- Allocation & Alignment to Project

Assess Stakeholders

- Hierarchy/Authority
- Roles/Skills
- Power of Influence
- Reaction to Change

Manage Stakeholders

- Survey/Feedback
- Change Readiness/ Issues
- Organizational & Process Alignment
- Performance Accountability
- Communication

manage them through the zipper curve as well as the response curve throughout the project life cycle.

The stakeholder list should be comprehensive. I remember leading a reengineering project for a Fortune 100 industrial manufacturer that was to implement new technologies and new processes across two divisions and five locations across the United States. When we first put our list together, we identified only twelve stakeholders. Most of them were people who would be directly involved in meetings. Once we reexamined the list and thought about the department heads, the entire system user base, the impact of the new processes on customers and downstream departments like customer service and accounting, our list grew dramatically to 180 stakeholders. The importance of this is that each one of these stakeholders were going to be affected—some to a small degree and some to a large degree, but all were going to be affected one way or another.

Whether you are involved in a small project with only twelve or so stakeholders, or in an enterprise-wide implementation (e.g., ERP), your list of stakeholders may be as large as a few hundred. By having a comprehensive list, you will be able to begin the process of putting together a real action plan for managing these stakeholders, which will help in achieving the overall success of your project. Think about a project that you are or have been involved in. Was everyone committed to the change? How many were in despair and could not get out of it? Were all stakeholders engaged throughout the project life cycle? If not, could this have been a contributing factor to the overall project success?

An example of a stakeholder list is shown in Figure 3-7. You can also use Exercise B-2 in Appendix B at the end of the book to develop your own stakeholder list. The list should include the name of the person, title, location, department, business unit, and percent allocation to the project (remember that they do not have to be allocated to the project, just be affected by it). You can add any other type of information that you feel would help you to identify and analyze them for the purposes of putting together an action plan to better manage them.

FIGURE 3-7. Sample of stakeholder list.

- **Anyone who is affiliated with a project can potentially have a positive or negative influence to the project.**

- **Stakeholders should be identified regardless if they have been allocated to the project.**

- **A comprehensive list can be used to manage commitment to the initiative.**

Example:

Name	Job Title	Location	Department	Business Unit	Allocation to Project
Sally Patterson	Planner	Chicago DC	Logistics	Piping	20%
Ed Riley	Plant Manager	Atlanta	Manufacturing	Piping	10%
Susan Right	Vice President	Chicago	Supply Chain	Piping	30%
Rob Trous	Receiver	Chicago DC	Logistics	Piping	5%

"HR"
KPI"

Metrics
to
measure
each
persons

① role + performance

Assess Stakeholders

Once the stakeholder list has been put together, the next stage is to assess each stakeholder by using a three-step process.

Step 1. Rate According to Power of Influence

First, you need to rate stakeholders according to their power of influence (see Figure 3-8). The power of influence means the stakeholders' ability to convince others in moving along either the positive or negative direction along the zipper curve we discussed above. The power of influence can have many different sources. The most common power of influence is the *positional power* of authority. Your boss, for instance, has positional power. As such, he could veto or support what you are trying to do based on his control of resources or control of budget, or just because he is the boss. Another such power of influence can be the technical or functional skills of a stakeholder. If this stakeholder is the only one or one of a few who possess a certain skill, they can control whether something gets done or is technically possible.

The same may apply to legal or policy power of influence. Suppose you need something to be approved by the legal or accounting department, and one lawyer or one accountant is not thrilled about your project. As such, she can use her power of influence to take a very conservative approach in getting something approved. This may be the case for getting a new product to market (e.g., a new medical device that needs FDA compliance or building permits for a new condo project). Their lack of commitment can be a negative influence and cause delays, or worse, prevent something from getting approved for your project. The same applies to other powers of influence, such as someone who controls communications and information, or someone who controls the external influence of credibility (e.g., an industry analyst or salesperson who interacts with customers).

Based on the power of influence, each stakeholder should be rated with a High, Medium, or Low rating—High being very powerful and

FIGURE 3-8. Assessing stakeholders: Step 1. Rate power of influence.

- **Step 1: Rate each stakeholder according to their power of influence**

  - High
  - Medium
  - Low

Power of Influence includes:

- Technical/Functional Skills
- Legal/Policy Control
- Positional Power and Authority
- External Influence or Credibility
- Access to Others or Control of Communications
- Informal Leadership
- Control of Resources

Example:

Name	Job Title	Location	Department	Business Unit	Allocation to Project	Power of Influence
Sally Patterson	Planner	Chicago DC	Logistics	Piping	20%	Med
Ed Riley	Plant Manager	Atlanta	Manufacturing	Piping	10%	High
Susan Right	Vice President	Chicago	Supply Chain	Piping	30%	High
Rob Trous	Receiver	Chicago DC	Logistics	Piping	5%	Low

Low being less powerful but still with some impact on your project. This can be easily done by putting a Low, Medium, or High rating next to each stakeholder whom you listed previously (see Figure 3-8).

Step 2. Rate According to Reaction to Change

The second step is to rate each stakeholder according to their current reaction to change (see Figure 3-9). This means determining how, given your perception and/or the perceptions of others, the stakeholders will respond to the change that this project will ask of them. A stakeholder's reaction will fall into one of three ratings:

1. *No Commitment*: Stakeholders are "on the fence" as to being a part of change and don't care either way whether this change takes place or not.

2. *Barrier*: Stakeholders have indicated that they do not want to be part of the change.

3. *Helper*: Stakeholders have indicated that they do want to be part of the change and will help make this change happen.

I have a couple of caveats about these ratings. First and foremost, these ratings should be as objective as possible. You should try to look at each person without letting any personal feelings about them as individuals get in the way. Whether you like someone or not should not influence how you rate them, and it will not benefit the project as a whole if you rate them harshly because you do not like them.

Second, try to come up with these ratings in a small group of individuals that are part of the project leadership team. This will help provide opinions about ratings for stakeholders whom you may not know personally and whom someone else does. This will also help in determining an objective rating without personal feelings. This small group typically should include team leaders, department managers, and trusted change leaders.

FIGURE 3-9. Assessing stakeholders: Step 2. Rate reaction to change.

- **Step 2:** Rate each stakeholder according to their current reaction to change:
  - **No commitment:** on the "fence" as to being a part of change; doesn't care either way.
  - **Barrier:** Has indicated that they **do not** want to be part of change.
  - **Helper:** Has indicated that they **do** want to be part of change.

Example:

Name	Job Title	Location	Department	Business Unit	Allocation to Project	Power of Influence	Current Reaction
Sally Patterson	Manager	Chicago DC	HR	Piping	20%	Med	No Commitment
Ed Riley	Supervisor	Atlanta	Manufacturing	Piping	10%	High	Barrier
Susan Right	Vice President	Chicago	Sales	Piping	30%	High	Helper
Rob Trous	Controller	Chicago DC	Accounting	Piping	5%	Low	No Commitment

- *Ratings are best done via objective feedback from group validation (group members typically consist of team leaders, department managers, trusted change leaders).*
- *Ratings should be kept confidential to the leadership team and revisited frequently.*

It should go without saying that the ratings for stakeholders should be kept confidential and should not be published or solicited beyond the core group. The worst thing that you can do is inform stakeholders how you and the project leaders rated them on their reaction to change. I certainly would not be happy if I found out that I had been rated as a barrier to the project. I am sure that you would feel the same way.

Now, when you rate each stakeholder, you should rate them in regards to their *current reaction* to change as well as the *target reaction* to change. Current means their current state. Target means the state to which you wish to get them based on your ability to manage them as stakeholders. In some cases, the rating for current and target may be the same. In other cases, you may be able to move a "barrier" to a "no commitment" rating. Moving them to "no commitment" is a good thing as long as you remove them as a barrier. A stakeholder who is a barrier is someone who will cause pain throughout the project life cycle, not only for you as project manager but also for your team. Getting them to move away from being a barrier is a good thing because at least it is in the right direction.

The target reaction to change allows the team to identify those stakeholders who you feel you can move along the zipper curve to the right (positive), and hopefully not to the left (negative). The important thing in putting together a rating for the reaction to change is that this reaction should be revisited frequently throughout the stages of your project. Things change as the project progresses, as do people and their reactions. By constantly monitoring a stakeholder's reaction, you as a project leader will be able to respond to their reaction and help keep them away from being a barrier to the project, or lessen their time in the despair stage of change. The result will allow you to keep focused on the execution of the project and its deliverables toward project success and achieving project business value.

Step 3. Categorize Stakeholders Based on Ratings

The third and final part of assessing stakeholders is to categorize them based on your ratings of power of influence as well as their reaction to change (see Figure 3-10). Putting them in categories will help in providing a holistic view of all of your stakeholders so that you will be able to put real plans in place for managing their commitment to change during and after the project. There are four categories of stakeholders:

- *Change Targets*. People who will need to change.

- *Change Leaders*. People with authority and position to help make change happen.

- *Change Influencers*. People who can influence change.

- *Change Advocates*. People who will help implement change.

Using the stakeholder category matrix in Figure 3-10, each category can be derived by finding the rating of power of influence on the Power-of-Influence column and then moving across the matrix so that the Reaction-to-Change rating can be found. The intersection of the two ratings will be the stakeholder category that can be assigned. For example, a stakeholder with a power-of-influence rating of "Medium" and a reaction-to-change rating of "Helper" is considered a change advocate. As another example, a stakeholder with a high power of influence and a reaction-to-change rating of "Barrier" is considered a change target.

It is the change targets and change influencers that we need to pay extra attention to because these are the stakeholders who can potentially derail our project. The reason for watching the change influencers is that they may be stuck in the middle of the zipper curve, and we are not sure whether they will be influencing our project negatively or positively. By managing the influencers along the positive side we will begin to move more stakeholders to the right of the zipper curve than to the left, which will result in a higher success rate for achieving our project objectives.

Where this all comes to light is shown in the graphic output in Figures 3-11A and 3-11B. This output is an example of an ERP implementation that was done across six departments and across six locations. In this output, you are able to view how many change targets or influencers

(text continues on page 117)

FIGURE 3-10. Assessing stakeholders.

- **Step 3:** From ratings, each stakeholder should be categorized by location and department so that change plans can be put in place for managing their commitment to the change process:

  - **Change Target**—People Who Will Need to Change
  - **Change Leader**—People with Authority and Position to Make Change
  - **Change Influencer**—Ppeople Who Can Influence Change
  - **Change Advocate**—People Who Will Implement Change

Example Category Matrix:

Power of influence	Reaction to Change		
	No Commitment	Barrier	Helper
High	Change Influencer	Change Target	Change Leader
Medium	Change Influencer	Change Target	Change Advocate
Low	Change Target	Change Target	Change Advocate

F I G U R E 3 - 1 1 A .   Sample stakeholder analysis output by location.

Category Type: Current

Project: 7778436

ERP Implementation

Stakeholder Categories by Department

FIGURE 3-11B. Sample stakeholder analysis output by department.

Category Type: Current   Project: 77784368

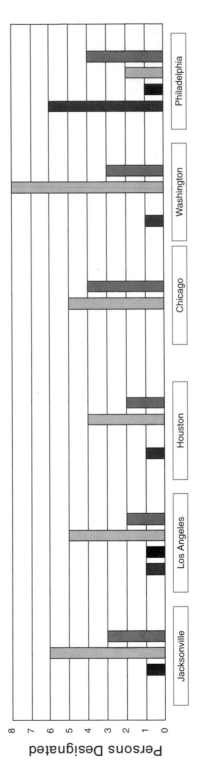

Stakeholder Categories by Location

ERP Implementation

Leader   Influencer
Advocate   Target

Change Target—People Who Will Need to Change
Change Leader—People With Authority and Position to Make Change
Change Influencer—People Who Can Influence Change
Change Advocate—People Who Will Implement Change

you have by location or department. The purpose of this holistic view is to tell you, as a project leader, where you will need to spend most of your time when managing stakeholders.

In the example in Figure 3-11, Philadelphia has a high number of change targets, but also a high number of change leaders. In this case I may leverage the change leaders to help manage those change targets. That will allow me to spend my time elsewhere in managing stakeholders, perhaps in Washington and Chicago, where I have a high number of change targets as well as influencers. My goal would be to move those influencers to the right of the zipper curve so that I can begin to manage those change targets and get them to also move to the right of the zipper curve. By looking at the graphic by department, I can also draw some conclusions. Given the number of influencers and targets, I will probably want to spend my time managing the stakeholders in the manufacturing and marketing departments.

The fact is that if you do your job by identifying a comprehensive list of all the stakeholders, you may have anywhere from fifty to maybe several hundred stakeholders to manage. In reality it is not possible to come in contact with or to personally be involved with so many stakeholders. These examples show how you may optimize your time and your team's time by focusing on certain departments, locations, and by leveraging others in the organization. The result will be your ability to better execute your stakeholder management plans. To obtain such output, you can use Microsoft Excel, which may require some extensive manipulating. I have also obtained good results with the ValueDriver4 product from ValueCurve Technologies (www.valuecurve.com). This is a simple Web-based product that walks you through the stakeholder management process to produce this type of output with a push of a button.

Manage Stakeholders

The third and final stage in the stakeholder management process is to manage stakeholders on a continuous basis. Stakeholders' reaction to change can vary over time, and so it is important to put a process in place to constantly monitor their readiness for change and be responsive to their needs. Managing stakeholders should encompass an execution of full-scale communication plans as well as accountability plans and incentives for those designated for driving change and achieving business case benefits. Stakeholders should also be assessed for skills and aligned within the organization to carry out the new process and technology changes. This will help in moving them toward the new way of doing things and getting them to drop their old methods.

Stakeholder Resistance

The important thing to remember as project manager and change leader is that you must be open to resistance. Resistance is normal and unavoidable when people realize they'll have to give something up. Understanding resistance and how to deal with it will help during those times of despair. Part of this is to allow people to express their feelings. Calling into question their feelings only encourages more resistance. Allowing stakeholders to surface and legitimize feelings of resistance provides for analysis, processing of feelings, and action planning to deal with them. The best way to think about resistance and to deal with it is to understand that there are two types of resistance.

The first type of resistance is positive, consisting of ways in which stakeholders will test the change they are asked to participate in. This may consist of their asking open-minded questions like, "How will you deal with this if that happens?" Other types of positive resistance may consist of disagreeing with or lobbying for alternative solutions, questioning the need for doing the project or activity, or just challenging the overall vision of the project.

These are all ways for a stakeholder to challenge the project, and you may need to spend additional time and effort to deal with the challenge. The best way to deal with this positive type of testing is to listen to the stakeholders and hear what they have to say. Support them in their logic by following it but drive them to an alternative solution that fits with your project objective or activity. Challenge them back. Doing your homework or involving key influencers early in the process is the best way to handle this type of resistance. Remember the accountant you involved while developing your business case, or the department head who sponsored your project, or even other influencers whom you involved during the early stages of the project? All of these people can help build the credibility for your project or for the activity that you are asking this resisting stakeholder to complete.

This will all help in making your case for change and show that you have thought through the alternatives to arrive at the solution you are proposing, and that it is supported by other key people as well. Don't be afraid to push back to this type of resistance in a manner that supports your case but also provides an opportunity for others to challenge you in a positive way.

The other type of resistance is more negative or results in sabotage. This is where the stakeholder does not come to meetings, pulls key people out of your workshops, ignores your project, or flat out "misses the plane" on purpose to avoid participation. This type of resistance goes way beyond questioning and moves to taking action to make matters worse for you and the project. The best way to deal with this type of resistance is to confront the situation as early as possible. Confront the stakeholders to find out why they are not participating or acting in a manner to sabotage your project. If you cannot resolve the matter with the stakeholder directly, then you must get help from your project sponsor or department head.

Most of the time this will improve the situation, but sometimes the problem continues. In addition you may need to solicit help from other stakeholders who may have influence over this person, like a friend or somebody who this stakeholder respects and who can help get them back on track. The last option, of course, is to remove this person from your project. Find others who can perform the same activities and get this person replaced. Not doing so will not only affect the activities that this person is to perform but will begin to affect the project team, who may start to question your ability to get the job done and lead the team to success. Take action with this type of resistance and make it quick and resolute. You will be happy you did.

Stakeholder Management Best Practices

The best practice for managing stakeholders is to accept stakeholders as they are (see Figure 3-12). Realize that it is hard to change yourself, let alone other people. Understanding where stakeholders are coming from will better equip you for taking the appropriate action to lead them down the path for change. In the case of resistance, don't be afraid to get other leaders or sponsors involved in helping to resolve the problem. As project manager your job is to resolve the problem whether you can do it yourself or with the help of others. A good leader will do whatever it takes to make things happen, so be open to getting help from others if needed.

When dealing with stakeholders, remember that you are most likely going to be dealing with emotions and sensitive situations that may be particular to the needs of a given stakeholder. As such, always ensure confidentiality to sensitive issues. This will not only build trust with the stakeholder but will also make you more approachable when others ask you to resolve surfacing issues. By taking an active approach, you as a project leader will have an easier time in dealing with stakeholders and managing them through the response curve as well as helping them get to the right (positive) side of the stakeholder commitment curve (zipper curve).

FIGURE 3-12. Managing stakeholders: best practices.

- **Accept stakeholders as they are.**
- **Get key leadership involved.**
- **Involve your stakeholders early.**
- **Ensure confidentiality on sensitive issues.**
- **Plan how to deal with and respond to each stakeholder.**
- **Help the stakeholders identify "what's in it for me."**
- **Communicate.**

Identifying stakeholders, assessing them, and putting an action plan in place to deal with them is the best way for gaining stakeholder commitment. Help the stakeholder define the "what's in it for them." This will be the logical question they ask at each stage during their journey through the zipper curve. Helping them answer that question will establish a common bond and demonstrate that you care and understand their particular needs from this project. Lastly, the single best thing you can do as a project leader to manage your stakeholders is to communicate, communicate, communicate! Letting people know where your project is going, where they stand, and what has been and will be accomplished is the single best way to engage team members, sponsors, and all stakeholders at large.

STAKEHOLDER COMMUNICATION

An intricate element of stakeholder management is communication. Effective communication, as simplistic as it sounds, is always the part of a project that seems to be missed. Whether stakeholders do not understand you, or you do not understand them, communication is always at the heart of many issues that arise on projects throughout and even after its implementation. Poor communication results in elevated emotions. Elevated emotions result in stakeholders moving to the left of the zipper curve whereby they become less committed to the change to be implemented by your project. The best way to increase your effectiveness in communicating with your stakeholders is to put in place a good communication strategy.

Communication Strategy

The basis of a good communication strategy starts with the development of a targeted communication plan among the project team, the steering committee, and the business communities. This plan should be able to satisfy the specific informational needs of the project team, the steering committee, the stakeholder community, and the business community at large throughout the life cycle of the project. For instance, the steering committee may only need to be communicated with on a monthly basis, whereas the project team may need weekly status meetings. In addition, you may decide that the business community may want to pull information from newsletters and project websites versus having information pushed to them via e-mails. The informational needs of different stakeholders may vary and your communication strategy should take this into account.

The idea of an effective communication strategy is to put in place a process for gaining commitment from the stakeholder community at large. Part of this process is to establish an effective two-way communication and the need for different messages over time. During your project life cycle, your needs for communication may vary. For instance, the early stages of your project will most likely require heavy communication up front to ensure that all stakeholders know what is going to happen, who will be involved, why your project has been initiated, and so on.

Once the project gets underway, the need for communication may lessen to the point of just providing periodic updates around key milestones, accomplishments, or issues. Consideration, however, should be made to not under- or overcommunicate. Many project teams get so excited about communicating that they communicate everything via e-mails and newsletters on a very frequent basis. Although the intent is to keep stakeholders informed, the process of overcommunicating may have a negative effect. Too much information may cause confusion as well as become annoying over time. The net result is that stakeholders will begin to ignore your messages and perhaps miss an important event or activity that they must know about or be involved in.

The opposite may occur in not communicating enough. Many projects start strong in their communication, but then stop or become less consistent in their communication over time. Communication becomes a less important issue when many other tactical activities begin to take place once the project really gets underway. This loss of frequency and consistency results in leaving stakeholders in the dark in terms of critical information and sets the stage for missed tasks and loss of buy-in over time.

Striking a balance between over- and undercommunicating is really where a good communication plan becomes invaluable. A good communication plan helps set realistic expectations as well as becomes a platform for quick issue resolution and decision making. This is key for dealing with project stakeholders so that their emotions can be kept at bay and their commitments can be maintained.

Communication Best Practices

Through my years of leading projects as well as going into bad projects in an effort to turn them around, I have found several best practices for a good communication strategy. The first is to keep messages simple and easy to understand and avoid empty messages. Don't just communicate to communicate. Send messages that are meaningful to the stakeholders and that are clear and concise.

The rule of thumb that I use in sending meaningful messages that can be understood is to be able to communicate the message to my wife. My wife is not involved in my business and does not understand the details of what I do, but if I can communicate to her the main points so that she can get an idea of what, when, where, and why, then my message is good enough to send. I am not advocating to run every message by your significant other, but the point is to keep it simple. Remember, most of the messages that you will be communicating will be to a broad audience with varied understanding of the topic. Some may even have only a slight understanding of the topic, like your significant other. Keep it simple, clear, and concise.

The second best practice is to keep communication consistent, frequent, timely, and relevant. As stated above, on typical projects communication starts strong but then drops off over time. I have had stakeholders on turn-around projects come to me and state that they have not heard anything about the project for months. This is bad. A conscious effort needs to be made on the part of the project team to communicate consistently.

The best way to do this is to ensure that stakeholders are informed around key milestones or deliverables. Share your successes. Inform them about the next steps and how they or their resources will be involved. Let stakeholders know that your project is still alive and kicking. Don't leave anyone out of the loop. Communication is about marketing. Marketing your project helps create buy-in as well as readiness for change. Don't miss the opportunity to market during the entire project life cycle.

The third best practice is to develop a cascading process of communication, involving all levels of management and influencers. Cascading communication can be from the top down as well as from the bottom up. Sometimes communication can be just as effective coming from lower level staff to management. Staff are involved in many meetings outside of your project, and with the right messaging they can help spread the word about your project. Think of it as a rumor mill; in this case, however, you are spreading a true rumor based on facts, and you control the message that is being sent.

The same is true for providing updates to your boss (or someone else's boss), which allows them to present a one-slide update at their staff meeting. This is a simple way to get people talking about your project on many different levels. Cascading your project message on many different levels is a great way to get your message out fast. Just remember to keep it simple.

As mentioned earlier, using different methods of communication is also important to ensure that your project message is properly heard and geared to the different audiences. Whether you use e-mail, project websites, conference calls, or any other method, each stakeholder or group of stakeholders may require different methods. One project in which I was involved, with 125 stakeholders across three divisions, used a communication method of sending newsletters to the business community of the three divisions. When we did a survey to monitor our communication process and obtain feedback (another best practice), we found that no one was reading the newsletters or liked receiving them. They preferred e-mails. Based on this feedback, we adjusted our communication method and discovered that the stakeholders were a lot happier because they were able to get to what they needed to know faster. This helped maintain their continuing support of our project during its life cycle.

Assign responsibility to communication. Because communications plans often get dropped during a project life cycle, assigning responsibility is a good way to ensure that this does not happen. Assignments can be made for particular stakeholders, groups of stakeholders, and even for methods of communication. For example, project managers are typically responsible for communicating to the project steering committee. Other team members or even those stakeholders identified as change leaders can also take an active role in executing a communication plan.

For example, I led a project that involved the realignment of an organization. Of course, this type of project often involves heightened emotions among stakeholders because of new reporting structures, new roles, and new responsibilities. During the stakeholders identification phase, we solicited a core team of change leaders, who were positioned in various key departments within the organization. None of them had positional power of influence, but they did have informal leadership roles that were very highly respected by others. Although we assigned responsibility to these change leaders to help in pushing the communication of key changes to the organization, we also solicited their help in pulling information from the organization on an informal basis to provide our leadership team information that we could use for developing our action plans. It was like having informal surveys that told the true story of how the stakeholders really felt about the changes we were implementing.

We leveraged these key change leaders by assigning them a role in the communication plan for providing and soliciting information that helped create a voice for the stakeholder community at large. The result was a more focused communication process that assigned accountability among key stakeholders, and it opened a channel of communication that was more timely and accurate.

The last best practice is, as was stated before, setting realistic expectations among stakeholders. Stakeholders must know what is expected of them. You, as project manager, should know what they expect from you, and, most importantly, all must know what the expectations are for the project overall. The beginning of the stakeholder response curve is all about their expectations. If the stakeholder expectations are too high, then the emotions of not meeting them will be greater when they experience any despair during the project life cycle. Of course, this will be harder for you manage and will create more issues for you to deal with at the time when despair occurs.

With all this said, it is your job as a project leader to manage expectation up front in the project as well as during all the stages of your projects. Always communicating with stakeholders and clearly articulating expectations is the best way to avoid pitfalls and help keep stakeholders on track to meeting project objectives.

Communication Process

It should be clear at this point that communication planning is an important part of stakeholder management. As such, putting together a communication plan follows a distinct process (see Figure 3-13). Once you have identified your stakeholders and assessed them, the communication process comes into play. The first step of the communication process is to identify the communication methods you want to use on the project as well as to establish the infrastructure you need to carry forth your communication plan.

There are many communication methods that projects use today, especially those that take advantage of the Internet. Some common communication methods are:

- E-mail
- Newsletters
- Project websites
- Conference calls

FIGURE 3-13. Communication planning process.

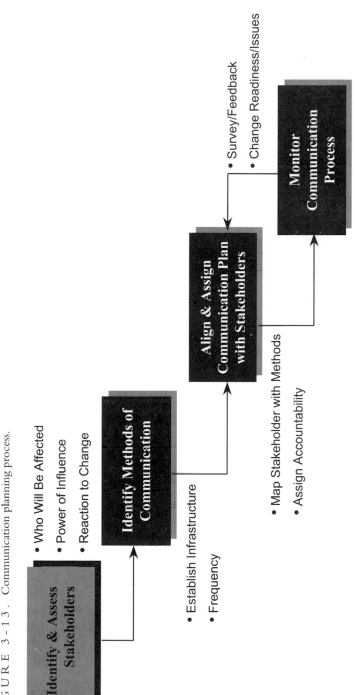

Identify & Assess Stakeholders

- Who Will Be Affected
- Power of Influence
- Reaction to Change

Identify Methods of Communication

- Establish Infrastructure
- Frequency

Align & Assign Communication Plan with Stakeholders

- Map Stakeholder with Methods
- Assign Accountability

Monitor Communication Process

- Survey/Feedback
- Change Readiness/Issues

- Workshops
- Web meetings
- One-on-one meetings
- Steering committee update meetings

The frequency of the types of communication methods may vary. For instance, a steering committee may meet monthly. Newsletters may be issued every other week, workshops may take place periodically or as needed during a specific stage of a project, and team meetings may be held weekly. Each method may require a different frequency, and each stakeholder or group of stakeholders may require a different method and frequency.

Once you have determined the communication methods and frequency, you should identify the infrastructure needed to carry them forth. For example, a project website or a Web meeting may require certain technology to host, maintain, or disseminate project information. Status meetings may require specific agendas that all attendees will need to adhere to. Project e-mails may require a standard format for communicating information. The communication infrastructure should become part of the planning phase of your project, where all project policies and procedures are established.

When establishing communication methods, keep in mind that there are different considerations for e-mail, telephone, and face-to-face communications (see Figure 3-14).

Communication by E-Mail

Understand that when sending e-mails, communication is 100 percent words. This means that the tone of the e-mail and the words that are written are the basis of the message and will be perceived as such. Choose your words carefully and be factual so as not to create unwanted emotions in the words that you write. E-mails can become a big waste of time if the words are not chosen carefully, and they can create a flutter

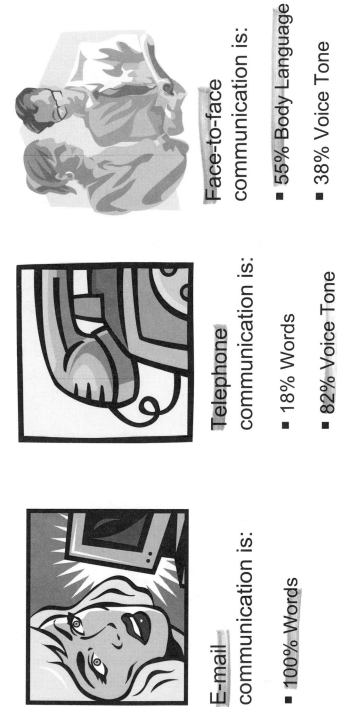

FIGURE 3-14. Considerations for communication methods.

E-mail communication is:
- 100% Words

Telephone communication is:
- 18% Words
- 82% Voice Tone

Face-to-face communication is:
- 55% Body Language
- 38% Voice Tone
- 7% Words

of responses. These responses in turn create more responses, which inevitably will involve others in the correspondence. The result is an e-mail trail that seems never to end, and all because the written words may have been misinterpreted. The best way to avoid endless e-mail trails and to address a negative or wrong interpretation of your e-mail is to pick up the phone and talk to the person directly.

Communication by Telephone

When talking to people on the phone, remember that communication is 18 percent words and 82 percent voice tone. Just the tone of your voice can send a message that leaves the person on the other end with a perception, whether positive or negative. Remember those days when your mother would ask you not to do something? She had a particular tone in her voice that would send a message beyond the words that she was speaking. Your perception of that tone sent you on course to respond by either following directions or challenging her directions. Depending on the type of child you were, the rest of the story is history.

The tone of your voice will send a message, whether intended or not. So be careful in your demeanor and smile while you talk on the phone. You will be surprised how well your smile comes through on the phone and how it will help communicate your message without creating a negative perception.

Face-to-Face Communication

Face-to-face communication is probably the best way to communicate; however, in today's world, it is often cost prohibitive. Traveling to various locations to meet with people takes a lot of time and money. With most budgets tight, face-to-face communication may not always be an option. Leveraging technology, however, can help. For example, video conferencing is a great way to cut expenses and time and still achieve some of the same benefits as a face-to-face meeting.

Regardless of how a face-to-face meeting is achieved, it is always a good idea to plan for a certain number of personal meetings and put them into your project budget ahead of time. As a result of the stakeholder assessment process done at the beginning of your project, you should have a good idea about which individuals or groups you should be meeting with, and at what locations. The purpose of the stakeholder assessment process is to determine which of these groups will need your attention most. Using this as an input to your communication planning is a great way to put an action plan in place and take advantage of the types and methods of communicating with your stakeholders.

Face-to-face communication is 55 percent body language, 38 percent voice tone, and 7 percent words. This means that your gestures are one of the keys to sending your message. As such, throwing your hands in the air while making a point is therefore not a good idea. Smiling while you speak and sitting up straight in a confident and professional manner probably is. There is a whole process of communicating through body language and linking it to words, which is called Neuro-Linguistic Programming (NLP). I won't go into the details about it here; however, if you are interested, more information can be found on the Internet. There are some great techniques that will help you as a project leader. The point is that the use of body language in balance with the tone and the words you speak definitely makes an impact into the way you communicate, which will help significantly in your overall communication with stakeholders.

Communication Plan

Once you have determined the communication methods and taken into account the appropriate considerations, you are now ready to begin putting together your communication plan. The communication plan is a document that maps a specific communication method for each stakeholder and assigns accountability for communicating with a stakeholder (see Figure 3-15 for a sample communication plan). In essence, a communication plan should indicate the stakeholder, location, department, and business unit they belong to, as well as the method, frequency, and

FIGURE 3-15. Sample communication plan.

Key information to be included in the communication plan:

Name	Job Title	Location	Department	Business Unit	Communication Method	Frequency
Sally Patterson	Planner	Chicago; DC	Logistics	Piping	Newsletter, Workshops, E-Mail	Monthly
Ed Riley	Plant Manager	Atlanta	Manufacturing	Piping	Newsletter, Workshops, E-Mail, One-on-One	Weekly
Susan Right	Vice President	Chicago	Supply Chain	Piping	Steering Committee, Newsletter	Monthly
Rob Trous	Receiver	Chicago; DC	Logistics	Piping	Newsletter	Quarterly

responsible owner of the communication. For example, you may request that the stakeholders communicate with you by providing status reports, in which case, you can add an additional column to your communication plan to store that information.

The communication plan should be an extension of the stakeholder identification worksheet that you previously put together (Exercise B-2). As such, each stakeholder or group of stakeholders identified should have a corresponding communication plan. The idea is not to get too fancy, but to keep it simple in terms of what you intend to communicate, when you intend to communicate, and who is responsible for communication to each stakeholder or group.

The communication plan and process should be monitored throughout the entire life cycle of the project. Not monitoring the communication process is as bad as not having a communication plan in the first place. Stakeholders require different methods of communication over time. What may be a good method and frequency today may not be as effective tomorrow. People get busy and priorities change. As a result, stakeholders may begin to ignore certain methods or even get annoyed by some of them. If you don't monitor the process and get feedback you will never know, and you'll assume that your communication process is working.

Communication Log

Monitoring the communication process should also include establishing a communication log. This log basically documents when the stakeholders were communicated with, what method was used, who communicated with them, what actions resulted from the communication, and any relevant documents that were used in the communication (see Figure 3-16). Typically the communication log is stored on a shared drive on a company server or some other place where your project team will have shared access. The concept is that any communication that occurs—a meeting, workshop, or conference call—will be placed in the communication log.

As project leader, you will need to define the usage of such a docu-

FIGURE 3-16. Monitoring the communication process.

- Communication is a continuous process that should be monitored to obtain stakeholder commitment to the change process.

- Communication is a critical foundation step in value realization.

- Communication plans should be directly linked to key stakeholders.

Example Communication Log:

Date	Communication Method	Audience	Topic	Responsibility	Action Items	Relevant Documents
9/12- 9/15/07	Workshops	Sally Patterson, Ed Riley, Rob Trous	Design Workshop	Team Leader	Investigate new process design.	SCM Overview Presentation
10/15/2007	Conference Call	Plant Managers	Discuss Project Plans and Staff Allocation to Project	Project Manager	Document plan and e-mail, talk to V.P. about staff conflicts.	Meeting Agenda

ment to ensure that it does not become cumbersome and tedious to manage. As with anything else, common sense should always be the rule of thumb, depending on your company environment and project. The key point is to use the log as a documentation vehicle so that communication as a process can be monitored and managed effectively. Think of the communication log as an information repository used for the purposes of tracking how well stakeholders are being managed. Over time you will then be able to go back and review how well the communication is working for specific stakeholders and groups. This is then the basis for readjusting the plan as the project progresses.

The communication log, just as the plan itself, are both good tools and techniques to jump-start your communication strategy. Other guiding principles should be considered for delivering your communication strategy. For example, always remember that communication is all about marketing the case for change. This means setting expectations upfront and managing those expectations throughout the project. Setting the proper expectations is all about ensuring that your project plan, objectives, and the "what's in it for me?" are clear and understood by all; otherwise your project is destined to fail from the beginning. Proper communication avoids this path and helps set the course for success.

Remember you can't achieve everything yourself. Getting others on board and committed to the change effort will only help matters. Communication is the silver bullet in this regard. Even if you find yourself not to be an effective communicator, get others on your team that are. In addition, put a solid communication plan in place to guide the process toward success.

Communication Feedback

Proactively monitoring the communication process by obtaining feedback is another good guiding principle. Feedback should be obtained both formally and informally. Formal feedback may include things like e-mail surveys or course evaluations for a training workshop conducted as part of your project. Feedback may also be informal, such as just asking a stakeholder about a recently attended project meeting. Don't be shy to ask for feedback. It shows stakeholders that you care about their input and feelings and that you consider their input to be valuable for making your project successful.

Asking people for their feedback is one of the easiest things to do but often never done. Perhaps we are afraid to hear the answers, or we just don't care. As a project leader you must care, because people are the key to your project success. If you don't get the feedback, you will never know how to adjust your plan.

Encouragement and Rewards

Another good communication guiding principle is to provide encouragement, support, and rewards. Encouragement of stakeholders through communication is a great way to motivate them. This motivation paves the way for creating buy-in and allows them to emotionally let go of their old ways of doing things. In doing so, they will be able to embrace the new ways, whether it is new technology, a new process or procedure, or adapting to new styles of management and organizational changes. Supporting stakeholders by establishing a two-way communication plan creates a platform for accepting the new ways of thinking. Support and encouragement builds confidence and allows them to test their own logic for working through the new process and get to the light at the end of the tunnel quicker.

As a project leader, you need to promote these new behaviors that your project requires by rewarding stakeholders for their actions and their thoughts. Whether you provide a bonus check, a day off, tickets for a dinner show—it does not really matter. What matters is that you as a leader and project manager have thought enough about your project stakeholders by providing them with some sort of reward. Whatever the size, any type of reward goes a long way. Celebrating successes, whether hitting a project milestone or just completing a small scheduled task, is a great way to publicize progress. Let everyone know of your team's success. Everybody loves a hero and everybody loves to be part of something successful.

CREATING ORGANIZATIONAL ALIGNMENT AND ACCOUNTABILITY

Once the Key Performance Indicators (KPIs) have been determined and the foundation enablers of Stakeholder Management and Communication have been put in place, the next step in the *Speed2Value*™ Road Map is Organization Alignment and Accountability. We discussed earlier how a stakeholder can have a positive or negative impact on your project. We must not ignore, however, that stakeholders themselves can also be positively or negatively affected. We talked about how stakeholders interpret change and how they can have an impact on your project. This was demonstrated through their progression through the zipper curve. What we will discuss now is the flip side of change by looking at how the project can affect the stakeholder.

THE IMPACT OF CHANGE

Quite simply, your project is about change. Whether you are changing a process, organization, or technology, your project will affect the way people or stakeholders work. This means that there will be new requirements for stakeholders. They may now require new skills—perhaps new skills for analyzing information, for using a new technology, or for working with other people, such as when stakeholders will now have to work as part of a team rather than as individuals. Or say your project is about implementing a new process that requires cross-collaboration among departments. This means that the work you perform will now become much bigger since there will be other people involved. A perfect example of this would be a project about implementing a new supply chain process.

The concept of a supply chain is about getting the right product to the right customer in the shortest possible time and cost. This requires working as a team to forecast the sales demand so that you know how much to produce and when; making the product at the least amount of cost; and finally shipping the product to the customer in the fastest possible time so that it gets there at the expected time and cost. Companies that cannot do this efficiently will lose market share to their competitors. With this said, in order to satisfy your customers in this supply chain example, many departments and people must work together. For example, the forecasting department needs to work with manufacturing, manufacturing needs to work with distribution, and distribution needs to work with the customer.

Implementing a new supply chain process requires that a holistic team be put in place to ensure a smooth flow of product and information. Suppose the new supply chain process was to be enabled by a new technology or tool that will facilitate the flow of information among the forecasting, manufacturing, and distribution departments. Stakeholders in this example may need to be trained in new team-based skills and in the upstream and downstream processes affecting their impact on each other.

Training for New Skills

Implementation of this new technology may require that each stakeholder acquire new skills for using the new tool on a daily basis. Certainly these new skills would be highly important to the overall success of the new supply chain process. Stakeholders must know how to use these tools, particularly when the new tool can help make them more productive and help consolidate information across the various departments. If the stakeholders are not properly trained or if they don't buy in to the new changes, then they'll end up going back to the old ways of doing their job. This, of course, would be counterproductive to the overall project objective of changing the way people work for the betterment of the whole.

Therefore, it is key to look at the skill requirements for each job. Sometimes individual stakeholders who need to be trained may not have the right aptitude for learning the new skills. If this is the case, you may need to look at hiring new people or realigning existing staff into these jobs so that the results from the training will be met. By looking at the job responsibilities and skills required for each stakeholder, you as project manager will be able to determine whether any of the players will need to be replaced.

Realigning the Structure

Continuing with this example of the supply chain project, we may find that improving the skills of the stakeholders is not the only requirement. As stated earlier, a new supply chain process means that many people need to work together in an integrated fashion in order to be successful. Looking beyond just changing the skills of the individual stakeholders or changing who the stakeholders are, a project of this type may also involve having to change the organizational structure overall.

For example, before this supply chain process reengineering project got started, each department (forecasting, manufacturing, and distribution) worked in complete silos. Each silo is a designated department, with its own boss, its own staff, and, most importantly, its own agenda for operating. If each department has its own agenda or departmental objectives, then it is almost impossible for a common goal to be achieved.

For instance, what if the forecasting department had a goal of forecasting what it *hoped* to sell rather than what it truly expects to sell? This would translate into the manufacturing department making more products than justified by demand, which would ultimately translate into additional manufacturing and storage costs. This is counterproductive to the manufacturing department's agenda, which is to make products that cost the company less. In this simple example we see that separate agendas impede the ability for the entire supply chain process to meet its overall objectives of getting the right product to the right customer in the shortest possible time and cost.

In an effort to mitigate having separate departmental agendas, it may be a good idea to realign the supply chain organization overall. What we discussed before is realigning the individual stakeholders in terms of their personal skill set. What we are talking about now is realigning the supply chain organization, overall. This means perhaps merging all three departments (forecasting, manufacturing, and distribution) into a single department called the supply chain. There would be one boss, an integrated staff, and, most importantly, a single agenda.

In addition, the reporting structure would change whereby cross-functional teams could be created. A team would consist of representatives from forecasting, manufacturing, and distribution to create a horizontal, process orientation rather than a vertical, departmental orientation. This reorganization inevitably would eliminate having separate departmental agendas and put in place a structure for having a common objective and achieving a common result: business value. This is a simple example of how people and organizations can be realigned in order to set the stage for achieving project value. However, having a single organization and people within it with the proper skill sets may not be the complete solution for achieving project business value.

ACCOUNTABILITY

The silver bullet comes when the people in the organization become accountable for the results and when there are incentives for them to achieve the results. Let's first focus on making people accountable for the results.

Earlier, we determined the Key Performance Indicators (KPIs) that were going to be used for the project. We also linked these KPIs to the financial and business performance drivers that show how the results would be achieved on the Project Value Driver map. The other side of the value driver map is linking these same KPIs to the stakeholders within the organization who will be accountable for delivering the results. To do this, you as project manager will need to put together what I call a stakeholder accountability plan.

Stakeholder Accountability Plan

A stakeholder accountability plan (see Figure 4-1) is basically a matrix for each stakeholder whom you identified earlier as part of your stakeholder management process. Within this matrix each stakeholder is linked to a particular KPI, the current baseline and future target objectives for the KPI, and a timeframe for achieving the KPI metric. Each stakeholder can be linked to more than one KPI. Also a KPI can be linked to a group or a team rather than an individual stakeholder. The key point is that there is a direct link between a KPI and a stakeholder and/or group of stakeholders. Linking it to an individual is always the best way to ensure achievement, but in some cases, such as the supply chain process project, it may be best to assign a KPI to a team. Either way, accountability will be accomplished.

Establishing a Baseline

Once the accountability link is made and documented on the stakeholder accountability plan, the next step is to determine the appropriate baseline and targets for achievement. First, we must determine the current baseline measure, or what we are currently achieving in terms of this KPI. Once this is done we can establish a realistic goal. One of the most common ways to establish a baseline for the KPI is to look at existing data.

FIGURE 4-1. Sample stakeholder accountability plan.

- **Assign KPI accountability to key stakeholders.**
- **Clearly Indicate current metrics, goals, objective and completion dates.**
- **Obtain communication and buy-in from management & owner(s).**
- **Link metrics to business objectives and original project business case.**
- **Track ongoing performance.**

Date Run:	03/24/2005					
Stakeholder KPI			**Current**			
		KPI	Measure	Goal	Objective	Completion
Andy Guevara	Manufacturing					
		Overall Equipment	50	100	Reduce to 20%.	04/29/2004
		Customer Complaint	11	0	Reduce overall complaints for Sears.	06/30/2004
Gillian Hale	Manufacturing					
		Production Yield	30,000	0	Reduce by 3,000.	09/30/2003
		Certified Suppliers	40,000	60000	Increase volume to supply base.	09/30/2003
		Customer Complaint	10,000	5000	Reduce overall complaints 50%.	09/30/2003
		Overall Equipment	20,000	15000	Failure reduction.	10/30/2003
		EDI Transaction per Supplier	50,000	69999	Increase transaction by supplier.	11/28/2003

The new KPI that you developed may be new because it never existed before or simply because it will now be calculated in a totally new way. Either way, existing historical data is a good starting place.

For example, let's go back to the supply chain project. Say, for instance, that one of our KPIs was forecast accuracy. Forecast accuracy can be calculated in several ways:

- Sales divided by forecast

- Sales less forecast divided by forecast

- Sales less forecast divided by sales

All of these calculations come up with different answers. If we are going to use a new measure of forecast accuracy for our KPI, we need to go back to historical data, in this case sales order data as well as forecast data, to determine what our current forecast accuracy is using the new KPI calculation. By doing so, we will have a good starting place for determining what our target goals can be. If we do not establish a solid baseline, the target goals will not only be unrealistic, but they will be cause for debate among stakeholders as to their legitimacy. As we discussed earlier, buy-in from the stakeholders is critical for the long-term achievement of the goals. Without buy-in, they will never focus on making sure that it will happen.

Calculation of the baseline measure is important and, to be honest, may take some additional effort to get the data as well as perform the analysis. The best way to streamline this process is to involve the stakeholders in gathering the data and either performing the calculations or at least verifying that they are correct. This will also help in getting the stakeholders to buy in.

Establishing the Target Goal

Once the baseline measure is established, you have a good starting point for determining the target goal. Perhaps a 50 percent improvement or an exact numerical goal to be achieved is in order. The target goal of a KPI should be realistic from the standpoint of being achievable, but also should not be so easy to achieve. Sometimes this is called a stretch goal, which means the KPI target can be achieved, but it will take a medium to high level of effort.

Stretching the stakeholder to realize the KPI result provides focus for the strategic project objectives while making it even sweeter when the goal is achieved. As such, the goal should be clear and concise. Being clear means that there is no ambiguity and that the stakeholder is fully aware of the objective and the meaning behind the metric. Whatever the target goal and objective, it should be documented clearly on the accountability plan and again discussed with the stakeholder who will be responsible for delivering the result.

Keep in mind that this discussion should be on several levels. One level is the individual stakeholders themselves, and the other is the executives to whom the stakeholder reports. By involving multiple levels, you begin to create not only the visibility for the KPI, but also the buy-in required to carry this KPI target goal forward on an ongoing basis. Coupled with this discussion is the time frame for achieving the target goal. The key here is that the stakeholder must be committed not only to deliver against the objective and target goal, but to deliver within a specific time frame. This is what begins to drive project value.

Creating an Action Plan

To support the target goal, an *action plan* should be put in place to ensure that the actual goal will be achieved (see Figure 4-2). An action plan is simply the steps that will be required to achieve the target goal. An example of an action step for a stakeholder could include the following: training, transfer of knowledge, increasing the data integrity of reports, or developing the team to utilize new skills. Whatever the action, there should be sufficient detail to describe the action steps required that will enable them to achieve the desired result and KPIs related to the project.

Now that KPIs have been developed as well as linked to stakeholders with appropriate action plans for achieving them, the next critical step is

F I G U R E 4 - 2 . Sample stakeholder action plan.

Stakeholder Action Plans
Project: 77784368 - Supply Chain Process Redesign

Name	Department	Completion Date	Management Action	Details
Gillian Ovitz	Manufacturing	12/24/2006 7/15/2006	* Develop new skills. Take training courses. * Transfer knowledge. Develop internal team and train the trainer for deployment.	
Tom Riley	Manufacturing	4/30/2006 4/30/2006	* Increase data & information integrity. * Develop new reports & mechanisms.	
Tonya Davis	Logistics	4/5/2006 4/9/2006	* Centralize and eliminate redundant process & systems. * Establish new production scheduling org. * Develop new or consistent performance measures. * Rush orders need to be defined. * Work with Purchasing on new contracts.	

to secure the buy-in from the top managers to support the actions to be taken by the stakeholder. Getting buy-in from the top managers started with the original business case that you put together and got approved. From the business case forward, you have been involving these top managers throughout the stakeholder management and communication process as well as by completing the *Speed2Value*™ task-level activities that were part of your tactical project plan. As such, it should be no surprise that you are now going back to these top managers to secure their buy-in for the most important part of the project: linking the KPIs to the stakeholders as well as to the action plans necessary to deliver the results.

This is the point in the entire *Speed2Value*™ Road Map process that establishes the full circle effect of linking the business case to the accountability within the organization. It is at this point that you ask the top managers to make the final commitment to your project and to its objectives that they originally approved. This final commitment involves putting in place a reward or incentive program that is tied to the KPI achievement.

REWARDS AND INCENTIVES

Tying rewards and incentives to KPIs is the knot that is required to not only realign behaviors, but finalize the stakeholder commitment to change, whether the stakeholders completely bought into the objectives or not. This is where the alignment to the top executives of the organization is established and the motivation of the front lines is secured. In other words, this is where "the rubber meets the road." There is no doubt that rewards and incentives are key motivators for driving an end result. These key motivators are important to be tapped into for overall project success.

Rewards and incentives can be established in many different ways. Those most to the point, however, are those that tie the achievement of the KPIs to compensation. Most likely a compensation plan that incorporates a bonus structure already exists within your company. This is a great way to tie in meeting your KPI target goal with a bonus. Why not? If the KPIs that you developed for your project are critical to realizing a benefit in terms of a business objective, then why would a top level executive fail to link achievement of these KPIs to compensation? If the rubber really is to hit the road, then this is where the top executives must demonstrate their commitment to the project and to the results that they expect to achieve from it.

The full circle again comes from your ability as project manager to tie the original business case to the project results to be achieved. The best way to establish this link is to tie your project into a program that already exists within your company. In this case, the company compensation is your best bet.

Short of incorporating KPI achievement into a compensation program, the next best thing is to offer some other kind of incentive or reward. This may include rewarding a team with an outing to a sporting event or with a party that includes spouses. It may also include providing paid days off or some sort of significant gifts. The idea is to offer an incentive to the stakeholders or group of stakeholders that provides something of value to them. Providing something of value is a motivator whether it is tied to compensation or not. Just assigning blind metrics to a stakeholder without providing them with an incentive of a personal benefit will have little impact. The lack of a framework for deriving a benefit to both the business and the stakeholders will automatically create a barrier to meeting your project objectives.

You, as project manager, will have enough barriers to overcome during your project life cycle without rewards and incentives being one of them. There are many types of rewards and incentives that can be offered in today's business environment. Don't be narrow in your thinking, think outside of the box, and think in terms of what would be of value to the stakeholders. Solicit input from others, including the stakeholders themselves. This again is a great way to obtain buy-in from stakeholders as well as from the top executives who must buy in to the reward and incentive program.

ESTABLISHING AN ONGOING PROJECT PERFORMANCE TRACKING PROCESS

Now that your project has been implemented, you as project manager have, it is hoped, met the tactical project objectives of being on time and on budget and within scope for its execution. But it is NOT time to move on! This is the stage where most projects end and where most projects fail to achieve the strategic project objectives of delivering value to the business. By operating within our new paradigm, we, as project managers and business leaders, now know that the project is not ending; it is just starting.

If we as business leaders agree that our project objective is to deliver business value, then completing the tactical deliverables of our project is just not going to cut it. We must stand tall as business leaders and project managers to recognize that this is the point where project value begins to roll out and where our success can be measured. Remember, however, that the 80 percent of the project effort that is spent on implementing the solution drives only about 30 percent of the business value. The other 20 percent of project effort will drive the remaining 70 percent of the business value. And this is where most projects fall short.

By following the *Speed2Value*™ Road Map, you as project manager were able to set the foundation for the achievement of project value. You developed a sound business case, determined the project value drivers, developed the KPIs and baseline metrics, and linked them to the key stakeholders with a reward and incentive program. If you have done your homework, there is no reason why you will not realize the maximum return from your project.

To realize this maximum return, you need to put in place an ongoing project performance tracking process. This tracking process will include:

- A timely and consistent reporting mechanism
- An ability to make project metrics visible within the organization
- A correction management process to ensure ongoing achievement of objectives.

REPORTING MECHANISMS

There are two main types of reporting mechanisms:

1. Business case scorecard
2. Project value booking

Business Case Scorecard

The business case scorecard is a way to directly link the original business case to the overall project objectives by focusing on measuring the four major elements of the business case on an ongoing basis (see Figure 5-1). The first element is the *project costs*. As highlighted in the original business case, these can include software costs, implementation costs, travel expenses, and any other types of costs detailed in the business case (even recurring annual costs). The scorecard provides a way to track what was approved in the budget compared to the actual costs incurred for each cost element. By tracking each cost element on an ongoing basis, both you as project manager and top management will be able to clearly see

FIGURE 5 - 1 . Business case scorecard: sample report.

Business Case Scorecard Report—Fiscal Year 2004

Project: 77784368—Supply Chain Optimization

Business Case Element	Approve/ Baseline	Estimated Value	Actual Value	Variance
Project Cost				
Hardware & Infrastructure	0	500	0	− 500
Software Licenses	0	100	0	− 100
Implementation Consulting	0	0	0	0
Custom Programming & Development	0	0	0	0
Travel & Expenses	0	30	0	− 30
Internal Resource Cost	0	0	0	0
Financial				
ROI		514%	83%	− 431%
Discounted Payback (yrs)		− 1.0		
Average Annual Savings		2,254	204	− 2,050
Net Present Value		8,560		
IRR		0.0%		
Delivery				
Schedule Start		7/7/2003	7/2/2003	− 3
Schedule Finish		4/9/2004	2/18/2004	− 37
Benefit				
User Satisfaction				
Increased Productivity				
Headcount Reduction				
Reduced Operating Expenses				
Reduced Billing Errors				

any variance, investigate the root causes, and put corrective actions in place.

The second element consists of the *financial impact measures*, such as ROI, payback, savings, NPV, IRR, or any other financial metrics used to justify the original business case. Again these are tracked on an ongoing basis by comparing what was approved against the actual results.

The third element measured by the business case scorecard is the *project delivery schedule.* The delivery schedule covers not only the project implementation dates but also the time frame for achieving the overall project objective. The time frame for achievement is based on the latest delivery date expected to be achieved by the stakeholders. This links directly to the KPIs projected to be achieved by each stakeholder.

The fourth element measured by the business case scorecard consists of the *soft benefits* that have been identified in the original business case. These include things that are hard to put exact measurements on, such as customer satisfaction, increased efficiency, or compliance with federal regulations. The business case scorecard is a great way to document these soft benefits as they occur so that they do not get lost over time and that proper credit can be given.

The purpose of the business case scorecard is to provide a way to capture data on an ongoing basis. It establishes not only benchmarks that are visible to the organization, but a mechanism for linking the original business case to the end result. The scorecard is a tracking mechanism that is not static. It is a "live" report that will change over time as new costs are incurred and new results are achieved.

Project Value Booking

The second type of reporting mechanism is what I call *project value booking* (see Figure 5-2). Project value booking is the ability to capture the actual values of the KPI metric while they occur, on a realistic and timely basis. Project value booking includes the actual value of the KPI metric, the date it is booked, the variance to the KPI target goal (both on an annual basis and for the period in which the KPI value booking occurs), and any

FIGURE 5-2. Project value booking: sample detail report.

Name	KPI	Target Goal	Actual Value Booked	Date Booked	Variance to Goal	Comments
Carl Sandor	Midwest Sales	$1M				
		Q1: $150k	$160k	31-Mar	$10k	Carryover from Last Year's Sales
		Q2: $300k	$250	1-Jul	($50k)	New Competition in Territory
		Q3:$300k	$275	1-Oct	($25k)	New Competition in Territory
		Q4:$250k	$350			
	Average Deal Size	$125k		$75k	($75)	Produced Bigger Discounts
	# of Sales Calls Closed	80%	60%	30-Mar	-20%	Focus on Last Year Closings
			78%	30-Jun	-2%	Better Response from System
			82%	15-Sep	2%	
Louis Truss	Sales Forecast Accuracy	95%	88%	17-Apr	-7%	New Forecast System Being Implemented
	Sales Order Errors	>2%	5%	30-Mar	3%	

comments related to the value of the booking. The idea is to capture as much information about the actual KPI metric as possible.

Project value booking can be done by the individual stakeholder or by a consolidation of information from various sources. Sources may range from information passed on manually to a reporting vehicle or to a more advanced business intelligence data warehouse.

In today's business environment, manual processes for capturing such data are rapidly becoming outdated. More often than not your company will have some sort of data warehouse in place that is used as a repository of capturing and storing information for the purposes of generating company-wide reports. A business intelligence data warehouse is a sophisticated repository of information storage and reporting that includes easy access to information as well as the ability to generate custom reports through advanced system functionality. The key aspect of a data warehouse, in general, is that it captures data from many disparate systems used within a company and ties the gathered information into one central place for reporting.

The reason that such a data repository is so important is that the actual data related to a KPI may indeed come from several different systems used within a company and can be reported on effectively through the use of one central data repository. For instance, sales data may come from an order management system, invoice data may come from an accounting system, and product planning data may come from a supply chain system. Instead of trying to get actual KPI information from each of these different systems, a central repository or data warehouse consolidates all of this information so that you can pull the data for KPI reports all from one place. This, in essence, helps automate the process of generating the project value booking concept as well as utilizes the business case scorecard. It also eliminates the need for capturing actual KPI data manually from stakeholders where computer systems were not used in the first place.

Project Portfolio Management

By having a central repository database in your company, many avenues can be pursued for imbedding project value as part of the overall project culture within your company. One such avenue could be the use of *project portfolio management* (PPM). Project portfolio management is a somewhat new concept that has been developing over the last ten years and has been gaining momentum, particularly within the last five years.

The idea behind project portfolio management is to be able to track projects similar to a portfolio of stocks, by monitoring each project along certain KPI criteria for the purpose of delivering value to the business. The concept is to view the portfolio of projects holistically and compare the projects to each other based on how each one is performing relative to its Key Performance Indicators.

Many of the KPI criteria consist of project risk or probability of success; tactical metrics such as schedule and budget; as well as financial criteria such as expected ROI and payback. There are many software products on the market today that help capture this type of data as well as report on it. Most of the PPM software products offered by market leaders like Primavera and ValueCurve Technologies offer a dashboard capability. This provides real-time visibility to KPIs by using a central repository concept of gathering and tracking project data, either within their own software or by integrating with other company systems. The software, however, is just an enabler to the overall concept of portfolio management.

The real bang for the buck with project portfolio management is the ability to analyze projects by comparing projects side by side during the business case justification process as well as during the ongoing tracking of the project during its life cycle. I must caution you, however, that many of the software systems today still focus more on the up-front business justification process to help determine which projects should be executed based on estimated project ROI, probability of success, and so on.

Many software programs still spend a lot of time with the analysis process to estimate the future achievement of results and little time with the accountability process of delivering the results once the project has been approved for execution and fully implemented. This is the area that the *Speed2Value*™ Road Map focuses on: delivering the remaining 80 percent of project results and tracking progress on an ongoing basis long after the project has been implemented. More and more of the software programs (e.g., ValueCurve.com), however, are moving in the direction of supporting the *Speed2Value*™ framework, which will help in enabling the new project paradigm of tracking and measuring project business value realization on an ongoing basis.

Portfolio management remains a strategic focus for managing projects and programs (groups of projects). The *Speed2Value*™ Road Map is the link between the strategy and tactical execution of a project and focuses on "how" the project value is actually to be achieved by following a provided process to manage the delivery of benefits. Together, portfolio management and the *Speed2Value*™ Road Map compliment each other in that PPM provides an enabler for gathering and tracking the information required to monitor the project value results.

One of the reports that I like to see from these types of PPM systems is a report on project value booked by business objective, as shown in Figure 5-3. Basically this report shows how much project value was booked from KPIs for each of the key strategic business objectives: business growth, cost reductions, speed and efficiency, and maintaining operations. This type of report is a great summary of how much business value is delivered by all of the projects within your project portfolio. By using a centralized project database, PPM software, or other specific KPI reports, you can put a timely and consistent reporting mechanism in place fairly easily.

METRICS VISIBILITY

The purpose of having a centralized database for capturing and reporting on project KPI data is to ensure that the information is easily accessible and can be gathered in a timely fashion. The caution, however, is not to get bogged down with too much information so as to be overloaded with many different or repetitive reports. As such, *project dashboards* have recently come to the forefront as a means for reporting the critical infor-

Booked Value by Business Objective

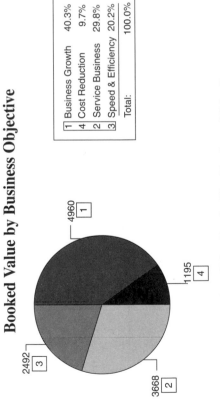

	Business Growth	40.3%
	Cost Reduction	9.7%
	Service Business	29.8%
	Speed & Efficiency	20.2%
	Total:	100.0%

Project Value Booked by Business Objective

	Business Growth	Cost Reduction	Service Business	Speed & Efficiency	Total
Customer Feedback Reporting	50.00	0.00	0.00	0.00	**50.00**
SOX Project	0.00	0.00	75.00	0.00	**75.00**
Increased Belt Speed	970.00	0.00	0.00	600.00	**1, 570.00**
On-Invoice Allowances	2, 850.00	0.00	0.00	1, 100.00	**3, 950.00**
Reduce C-11 Batt Length	325.00	890.00	3, 343.00	77.00	**4, 635.00**
Supply Chain Optimization	765.00	305.00	250.00	715.00	**2, 035.00**
Total	**4, 960.00**	**1, 195.00**	**3, 668.00**	**2, 492.00**	**12, 315.00**

mation. A project dashboard is like a dashboard in an automobile, where a few gauges report on only the important measures required to keep the car running successfully, such as speedometer, oil gauge, or fuel gauge. Similarly, a project dashboard focuses on the schedule, budget, ROI, value bookings, or any other KPI that is critical to project success.

The idea of the project dashboard is to keep critical information visible and timely, so that project KPIs will always be on the minds of key stakeholders and top executives. This is where the old adage comes in: "You manage what you measure." People tend to focus on things that are visible to others, especially their boss. The good thing about having project KPIs visible is that it does not just measure poor performance against a project KPI. What if your performance is good? Wouldn't you want everybody to see how great you are doing? This would be a good thing for your boss to see, especially if your performance against a KPI is a basis for a reward like a raise or bonus.

Keeping project performance visible within your organization does not have to come in the form of a project dashboard or part of a centralized system. Keeping KPI metrics visible can be as simple as a report or an e-mail distributed to key people within your organization. Keeping KPI metrics visible can also be done via company newsletters, websites, or even posters on a wall in a cafeteria or common corridor.

For instance, say that you are implementing a new process to help reduce the number of order entry errors by an inside sales organization. One way to keep the KPIs visible would be to post, on a weekly or monthly basis, the number of order entry errors versus the target goal reduction on a wall within the sales department. This would make them visible to everyone walking through the department as well as to the stakeholders responsible for achieving the KPI target goal. Keeping the KPI visible reinforces their importance. Every day stakeholders will walk into their department and see the number of order entry errors versus the target goal. Every day the stakeholders will think about how they can contribute to achieving the KPI goal. Having a KPI metric visible, particularly as it relates to a target goal, is a motivator not only for the individual stakeholders but for the order management team overall.

Drawing attention to a KPI metric is important for the leadership team, the individual stakeholder, and others in the organization to be able to see how important it is to manage what you measure. Hopefully, increasing the visibility and communicating the performance of KPI metrics will catch on and be used to effectively manage your project, your business, and the people who make things happen within your organization. Just being visible, however, is not the end of the story.

CORRECTION MANAGEMENT

Visibility to a KPI in comparison to its target goal draws attention to the matter at hand. The matter at hand can be one of two things. Either the stakeholder or team is meeting the target goal, or not. Meeting the target goal is the easy part. In this case, congratulations to those involved is in order and the appropriate rewards, such as bonuses or nonfinancial recognition, should be given to reinforce the behavior for achieving the objective. The difficult matter is when the target goal is not being achieved. In this case, a corrective action plan must be put into effect to help get the project KPI back on track toward the target goal. Part of the corrective action plan is to determine why the project KPI target is not being achieved. A good place to start in investigating the root cause is to review the original action plan for achieving the KPI. Remember the action plan was put together to address the key activities as well as the time frame for when these activities needed to be completed. A quick review of the stakeholder action plan will reveal whether the activities were actually done and whether they were done in the time frame specified. Any deviation from the intended stakeholder action plan will need to be addressed by identifying the barriers causing the compliance failure.

The issues identified should then be brought to the attention of the key project sponsors who have been supporting the project from the beginning. These are the very sponsors who approved your project for implementation and who committed to the reward and incentive program that was put in place for achieving the KPI objectives. Project sponsors can help in removing the barriers and in developing a corrective action plan.

Project sponsors typically are the executives with positional power and political influence within the organization. They also control resources and budgets. Barriers for not achieving project KPI objectives are often caused by lack of resources or changing priorities or focus within a department or team. If your project has been properly linked to the strategic objectives of the company, and if the value drivers and KPIs have been properly bought into by the right stakeholders (including the sponsors), then removing such barriers should be a no-brainer. As previously discussed, project sponsors play a critical role in getting your project approved, helping with the project implementation, and managing the project stakeholders throughout the entire project life cycle. They are critical in helping to maintain an ongoing performance management process for the purposes of achieving project objectives.

Your project does not end with the project implementation. That is just the beginning. The foundation that you established with the *Speed2-Value* Road Map is in full swing at the implementation of the solution. This is when the stakeholders grab hold of the new processes, tools, and structure that you put in place, and this is where the support that you have been rendering throughout the process is embraced.

CONCLUSION

Driving project success starts with putting in place a process that is strategically focused on achieving the overall project objectives set out in the original business case. Following the *Speed2Value*™ Road Map process is your best way to ensure success in delivering project value and benefits to the business. We followed this process from start to finish starting with the business case. It is the original business case that sets the stage for what the project benefits are and how they will be achieved. Within the business case we:

- Documented the areas that could be improved for driving the business benefits
- Argued the justification based on strategic fit with the organizational objectives
- Identified project risk
- Estimated project cost and return on investment
- Laid out an implementation plan for achieving overall project success

While going through the process of getting our project approved, we strategically navigated the business case influencers and supporters to obtain executive level sponsorship. This sponsorship is the foundation your project steering committee uses to execute your project plan. Later this same level of sponsorship was drawn upon in order to secure final commitment from key stakeholders that are tied to the various value drivers of your project.

Once your project was approved, we conducted a detailed project value driver mapping all of the financial drivers and operational levers to link the original business case to the benefits to be achieved. From this value driver map, we determined the operational levers, or Key Performance Indicators, and used them as the first step in establishing the foundation for measuring project success.

After the KPIs were developed, we established a Stakeholder Management process that identified the people who would have an impact on our project, either positively or negatively. At the same time, we put in place a communication process that would keep the lines of communication open and help increase our chances of obtaining the commitment of the stakeholders throughout the project life cycle.

Once the stakeholder and communication process was established we then aligned the organization for the proper skills and teams needed to carry out the project objectives. We put in place a reward and incentive program that linked to existing compensation policies and offered a "what's in it for me?" approach to all stakeholders. This approach of rewards and incentives set the foundation for ongoing achievement of project value once the tactical project implementation was completed. To measure the ongoing achievement of project value, we put in place a business case scorecard as well as other mechanisms to capture KPI data and measure our ongoing project performance. We used portfolio management concepts whereby our project became one of many projects within a company portfolio being tracked for ongoing performance.

In essence, the process for achieving project business objectives starts at the initial planning stages for the project and carries through to the final project implementation, after which it is incorporated in the ongoing operations of the business. Project value must be part of the overall project plan, with distinct activities to be completed. To be achieved, project value must be linked to the tactical execution of a project.

When this is done from the start of your project, you will no doubt be able to engage the right stakeholders to be successful. In addition, you will be able to call upon those project sponsors to support your endeavor when it really counts: at project completion. It counts at the end of your implementation because that is the stage when the project benefits are to start rolling in and when the stakeholders are to be held accountable for the results. With the right KPI metrics linked to the proper stakeholders, the right tracking system to measure the results, and the right project sponsorship to reward the achievement, project success is not too far away.

Going beyond "on time and on budget" is the only way to achieve real project success. This is your chance to shine above the rest. Executing your project with a business-value mindset is the way that you can begin delivering the results. Maximizing project value is about defining your project success road map, managing the execution process with project value in mind, and measuring your project success for maximum return.

PROJECT BUSINESS CASE

EXERCISES

Appendix A contains six exercises to help support the concepts presented in Chapter 1, Defining the Project Business Case and Getting Buy-In from Top Management. Each exercise is meant to trigger your thought process as well as walk you through the basic concepts of the key points within that chapter. Note that each exercise can be enabled through a variety of automation mechanisms.*

EXERCISE A-1: PROJECT INITIATION DOCUMENT

The first exercise is developing a Project Initiation Document (PID). As we learned, the PID is a document that begins the business case development process by formally documenting the project objectives and description, leadership and organization, and overall project scope. For a project that you are currently working on or will be involved in, complete the PID form.

*ValueCurve Technologies, Inc., offers a fully automated business case and stakeholder management system called ValueDriver4. For more information, go to www.valuecurve.com.

Exercise A-1: Project Initiation Document

Project Name _____

Project Description _____

_____

_____

Project Objective _____

_____

_____

Business Objective _____

_____

_____

Project Sponsor _____

Sponsor Department _____

Project/Program Manager _____

Project Category _____

(e.g., business process, new product development, research)

Project Locations 1) _____

2) _____

Project Business
Units
1) _____

2) _____

Project Stakeholder
Departments
_____

_____

Enter Project Schedule

Milestone Stages	Planned Start Date	Planned Finish Date
1)		
2)		
3)		
4)		

Project Approvers
_____

_____

(e.g., controller, director of finance, director of IT)

EXERCISE A-2: INITIAL ASSESSMENT

From the PID, begin the project initial assessment by using the Initial Assessment form. Describe the current situation or environment for your project. Is there a need for change that your project will address? Next, identify any potential barriers for achieving the goals of your project. Document the soft benefits for your project in terms of things that may not be easily measured (e.g., regulatory compliance, increased employee morale). Add any comments or assumptions about the benefits that you expect to achieve.

Exercise A-2: Initial Assessment

Description of Current Situation (need for change)

_____

_____

_____

_____

_____

Potential Project Barriers

_____

_____

_____

_____

_____

_____

Select Soft Business Benefits (customer satisfaction, product quality)

_____

_____

_____

_____

_____

Benefit Comments

_____

_____

_____

_____

_____

EXERCISE A-3: RISK ASSESSMENT

Using the Risk Assessment form, identify the risk factors under each of the project risk types (delivery risk, business risk, and technical risk). Risk factors are used to identify the types of risk associated within a given project (e.g., delivery risk may include risk factors such as budget, scope, schedule, and delivery resources). For the purposes of this exercise and in the spirit of making the calculation easy, we have assigned equal importance to all risk factors with a rating of 3. As such, the weight factor becomes a rating of 10 for each of the risk factors. Since the weight factor is already determined, rate the impact of each risk factor using a rating from 1 to 3.

For the impact rating, 1 equals low, 2 equals medium, and 3 equals high. The higher the impact rating, the bigger the impact on the project success if the risk is not mitigated. Similarly, rate the probability for each risk factor using a rating of 1 to 3. For the probability rating, 1 means it's unlikely that the risk factor will occur, 2 means that it is possible that the risk factor will occur, and 3 means that the risk factor is likely to occur. After you have determined the impact and probability rating, calculate the total rating for each risk factor by multiplying the weight by the impact and probability rating. Once you have calculated the total risk rating for each risk factor, sum all of the totals to get the overall project risk rating. Using the overall risk rating number (sum), find the corresponding risk rating description in the risk rating matrix in the assessment form (e.g., high, moderate, low).

Exercise A-3: Risk Factors and Ratings

Part 1

Type of Risk	Importance (Rate 1 = Low to 5 = High)	Wt. %	Impact (Rate 1 = Low / 2 = Medium / 3 = High)	Probability (Rate 1 = Unlikely/ 2 = Possible /	Total Rating
Delivery Risk					
	3	10 ×	×		=
	3	10 ×	×		=
	3	10 ×	×		=
	3	10 ×	×		=
Business Risk					
	3	10 ×	×		=
	3	10 ×	×		=
	3	10 ×	×		=
Technical Risk					
	3	10 ×	×		=
	3	10 ×	×		=
	3	10 ×	×		=
	Total Importance	100		**Overall Project Risk Rating**	

Note: Multiply Importance Weight % × Impact × Probability to get a Total Risk Rating for your project.

Part 2

Determine where your Overall Project Risk Rating falls to rate your project risk.

500 & above = Very high project risk

> Very heavy impact on project success and risk very likely to happen if not mitigated.

400–499 =   **High project risk**

Heavy impact on project success and risk likely to happen if not mitigated.

300–399 =   **Moderate project risk**

Some impact on project success but risk not likely to happen.

200–299 =   **Low project risk**

No significant impact on project success and risk not likely to happen.

100–199 =   **Very low project risk**

No significant impact on project success and low probability of project failure.

Total Project Risk Rating _____

Implementation Plan & Assumptions

_____

_____

_____

_____

_____

EXERCISE A-4: RESOURCE REQUIREMENTS

Using the Resource Requirements worksheet, identify the project roles that will be required for implementation. Then, identify whether the resource role is "internal" to your organization or "external," such as a consultant, and mark the form accordingly. Next, estimate the number of hours per month the resource role is required to work on the project (a typical month has a total of 160 hours available). After that, multiply the total hours for each resource role by the standard rate to get the Estimated Total Cost for each resource role (for this exercise, use an internal rate = $50/hour; external rate = $100/hour). Finally, sum the Total Costs to get the Overall Resource Costs for your project. Document any resource assumption in the space provided on the form.

Exercise A–4: Resource Requirements

Enter Estimated Monthly Hours

Role	Type (Internal or External)	Mar	Apr	May	June	July	Aug	Sept	Oct	Nov	Dec	Jan	Feb	Mar	Estimated Total Hours	Estimated Total Cost
Example IT Manager	Internal	4	8	25	36	40	20	8	8	5	5	5	0	0	Add up months Mar thru Mar 164	Internal × $50 External × $100 Hours × Rate $8,200
														Overall Resource Cost	

Resource Assumptions

EXERCISE A-5: TOTAL PROJECT COST ESTIMATE

Using the Total Project Cost worksheet, identify the types of costs your project will incur (e.g., travel expenses, hardware, software). Next, estimate the monthly cost for each cost element. Then, add cost estimates for each element to get Total Costs. Add all total costs to get Sum Total Project Costs. From the Resource Cost worksheet, transfer Total Resource Cost in the box provided. Add Sum Total Cost to Resource Total Cost to get Overall Project Cost. Document project cost assumptions in the space provided on the form.

Exercise A-5: Total Project Cost

Enter Monthly Cost Estimates

Cost Metrics (All values in $ thousands)	Mar	Apr	May	June	July	Aug	Sept	Oct	Nov	Dec	Jan	Feb	Mar	Total Costs
Example Travel & Expenses	4	8	25	36	40	20	8	8	5	5	20	30	18	227

Total Project Cost		
+	Overall Resource Cost	
=	Overall Project Cost	

Project Cost Assumptions

EXERCISE A-6: FINANCIAL RETURN

Using the Financial Return worksheet, identify the types of savings your project will achieve (e.g., customer complaint savings, inventory reduction). Next, estimate the savings per month for each savings category. Add savings estimates for each category to get Total Savings Impact. Add all Total Savings Impact to get Sum Total Project Savings. Finally, calculate ROI using the formula:

$$\text{(sum total project savings } - \text{ overall project costs)}/$$
$$\text{overall project costs} \times 100$$

(Note that the overall project cost was determined in Exercise A-5.) Document Financial Return Assumptions in the space provided on the form.

Exercise A-6: Financial Return

Monthly Financial Impact Data by Category

Financial Impact Data (All values in $ thousands)	Mar	Apr	May	June	July	Aug	Sept	Oct	Nov	Dec	Jan	Feb	Mar	Total Savings Impact
Example Reduced Customer Complaints	4	8	10	12	12	10	8	8	5	5	5	5	5	97

ROI Calculation [ ]

ROI Calculation:

$$\frac{\text{Sum Total Project Savings} - \text{Overall Project Cost}}{\text{Overall Project Cost}} \times 100$$

Financial Return Assumptions

STAKEHOLDER MANAGEMENT

EXERCISES

Appendix B contains five exercises to help support the concepts presented in Chapter 3, Achieving Project Value Through Stakeholder Management. Each exercise is meant to trigger your thought process as well as walk you through the basic concepts of the key points within that chapter. Note that each exercise can be enabled through a variety of automation mechanisms.★

EXERCISE B-1: SHARING YOUR EXPERIENCE WITH CHANGE

For this exercise, choose a project that you have been involved in or will be involved in that required or will require some sort of change. The change could be related to process, technical (systems, products), or organization. Once your project has been chosen, describe a change objective of the project. Then describe the type of change that was or will be required. Document what went well and what did not go so well with

★ValueCurve Technologies, Inc., offers a fully automated business case and stakeholder management system called ValueDriver4. For more information, go to www.valuecurve.com.

the change that the project required. How did the behavior of the people involved with the project influence the change that was required by the project?

Then document what you learned from the change experience. Ask others within your company about a change experience that they had. You may find that their experience had similar themes to yours. The idea is that change affects people and that people can also influence the change that is required of them. If not managed properly by you as project manager, the project objectives and business value will be much harder to achieve.

Exercise B-1: Sharing Your Experience with Change

Project Name   _____

**What was the change
objective?**   _____

                                    _____

                                    _____

**What type of change
did the project
require?**   _____

                                    _____

                                    _____

What went well?   _____

                                    _____

                                    _____

What didn't go well? _____

_____

_____

**How did people's
behavior influence
the change?** _____

_____

_____

**What did you learn
from the experience?** _____

_____

_____

_____

EXERCISE B-2: IDENTIFYING STAKEHOLDERS

For a project that you are working on or will be working on, identify at least twelve stakeholders. Remember that a stakeholder is defined as anyone who could influence your project either positively or negatively. When identifying your project stakeholders, make sure to reach beyond those who are directly involved in your project, such as team members. Even if not directly involved, a stakeholder can have a huge impact in the overall success of your project.

Start by first identifying all of the departments (start with three to understand the concept) that will be affected by your project change. These departments may be users of new processes or systems, customers, or groups of stakeholders. Once departments or groups have been identified, list the names, job titles, location, and business unit that the stake-holder belongs to. Remember to identify at least three stakeholders under each department or group.

Next, define how much time, if any, will be allocated for each stake-holder's required participation during the project life cycle. Participation may range from none, to little (attending meetings or workshops), to full time (team members). Not every stakeholder needs to have a time allocation.

Exercise B-2: Identifying Stakeholders

Department Name	Stakeholder #	First & Last Name	Job Title	Location	Business Unit	% Allocated
	1					
	2					
	3					
	4					
Department Name	5					
	6					
	7					
	8					
Department Name	9					
	10					
	11					
	12					

EXERCISE B-3: ASSESSING STAKEHOLDERS

Once all of your stakeholders are identified, rate each stakeholder according to their Power of Influence in Column 3a of Exercise B-3, Part 1. Remember that the Power of Influence includes technical skills, their ability to influence policy or legal control, positional power within the organization, access to others in regard to controlling information, informal leadership, and the ability to control resources. Give each stakeholder a rating of High, Medium, or Low according to their Power of Influence and enter their rating in Column 3a. The number of the stakeholder should correspond to the number used in Exercise B-2.

After you have entered the Power of Influence rating, assess each stakeholder according to both their current and their target Reaction to Change. The *current* Reaction to Change is an assessment by you (or your leadership team, for objectivity) of how you think each stakeholder will react to the change that will be required of them.

Their reaction will be one of three: no commitment, a barrier, or a helper. *No commitment* means that they are "on the fence" and don't care either way about the change resulting from the project. It also means that they are caught between the zipper on the zipper curve discussed in Chapter 3. *Barriers* are stakeholders who have indicated that they *do not* want to be part of the project change effort. *Helpers* are stakeholders who have indicated that they *do* want to be part of the change effort. Enter your assessment in Column 3b.

Using the same criteria, assess each stakeholder based on their *target* Reaction to Change and enter the rating in Column 3c. For instance, a stakeholder who is a barrier currently may not necessarily be a barrier in the future. If you can put in place a good stakeholder management process, you may be able to get them to be helpers. In some cases this may be possible, in others your goal may be just to get them to a "not committed to the change" rating. This will at least move them from having a negative impact on your project. With stakeholders who are currently assessed as barriers and who will always be assessed as barriers, at least you know what is possible and will be able to put in place the appropriate stakeholder management process.

Once you have completed your current and target assessment ratings, categorize each stakeholder as one of the following:

- *Change Targets*. People who will need to change.

- *Change Leaders*. People with authority and position to help make change happen.

- *Change Influencers*. People who can influence change.

- *Change Advocates*. People who will help implement change.

Each category can be derived by using the Category Matrix below. Using the Power of Influence rating from Column 3a and the Reaction to Change rating from Column 3b, find the box in the matrix where both ratings intersect. The intersection of the two ratings will be the stakeholder category.

Reaction to Change

Power of Influence	No Commitment	Barrier	Helper
High	Change Influencer	Change Target	Change Leader
Medium	Change Influencer	Change Target	Change Advocate
Low	Change Target	Change Target	Change Advocate

For example, a stakeholder with a Power of Influence rating of *Medium* and a Reaction to Change rating of *Helper* is considered a change advocate, and a stakeholder with a *High* Power of Influence rating who is assessed to be a *barrier* is considered a change target. Document the appropriate stakeholder category in Column 3d. Also in Column 3d, calculate the number of change Leaders, Advocates, Influencers, and Targets (L = Leader, A = Advocate, I = Influencer, T = Target).

Now complete the Stakeholder Assessment Chart in Part 2 of Exercise B-3. Based on the total number of stakeholders for each category and department, place an "X" in the appropriate box above each department shown. For instance, if you have four stakeholders categorized as "advocates" for your first department, place an "X" at the horizontal intersection above the letter "A" and the number 4 that appears on the vertical axis of the chart. This will give you a holistic view of your stakeholder assessments across each department. From there you will be able to put the appropriate stakeholder management plans in place.

Exercise B-3. Part 1: Assess Stakeholders

Stakeholder #	Column 3a Power of Influence (Low, Medium, High) Use this column to calculate Column 3d	Column 3b Current Reaction to Change (No Commitment, Barrier, Helper) Use this column to calculate Column 3d	Column 3c Target Reaction to Change (No Commitment, Barrier, Helper)	Column 3d Stakeholder Category (Leader = L, Advocate = A, Influencer = I, Target = T) Using the Category Matrix, determine the type of category from Columns 3a and 3b.
Department				
1				
2				
3				
4				

DEPARTMENT TOTALS			
L	A	I	T

Department	5					DEPARTMENT TOTALS		
	6					L	A	I	T
	7								
	8								

Department	9					DEPARTMENT TOTALS		
	10					L	A	I	T
	11								
	12								

Exercise B-3. Part 2: Stakeholder Assessment Chart

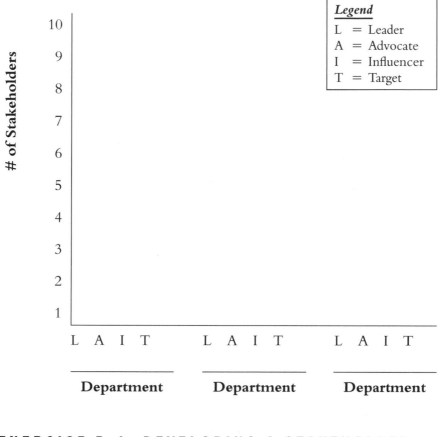

# of Stakeholders

10

9

8

7

6

5

4

3

2

1

L A I T   L A I T   L A I T

Department   Department   Department

Legend
L = Leader
A = Advocate
I = Influencer
T = Target

EXERCISE B-4: DEVELOPING A STAKEHOLDER COMMUNICATION PLAN

For each stakeholder number indicated from your stakeholder identification exercise, document the method of communication you plan to put in place for each stakeholder (e.g., meetings, one-on-one, e-mail, conference calls). Then define the frequency of each communication method that is required (e.g., monthly, weekly, as needed). Once these two items are documented, identify the responsible owner for making sure that each communication method and frequency occurs.

Exercise B-4. Develop Communication Plan

Stakeholder #	Method of Communication	Frequency of Communication	Responsible Owner
1			
2			
3			
4			
5			
6			
7			
8			
9			
10			
11			
12			

EXERCISE B-5: ESTABLISHING STAKEHOLDER ACCOUNTABILITY

For each stakeholder indicated in Exercise B-2, identify the Key Performance Indicator (KPI) metric. Remember that not all stakeholders for your project will require a metric. For the ones that do, however, document the metric, the target goal, the objective of the KPI, and an estimated completion date for achieving the KPI. The result of this accountability plan will be a document that can be used to hold stakeholders accountable for achieving the results. This plan can serve as the baseline for achievement and be referred to during the project life cycle and beyond as the project value is to be booked, as discussed in detail in Chapter 5.

Exercise B-5. Establishing Stakeholder Accountability Plans

Stakeholder Number	Current Metric	Target Goal	Objective	Completion Date
1				
2				
3				
4				
5				
6				
7				
8				
9				
10				
11				
12				

KEY TERMS

Business Case—A project justification document that outlines a project proposal for authorized funding, resources, and implementation.

Business Case Scorecard—The business case scorecard is a way to directly link the original business case to the overall project objectives.

Deployment Schedule—The key milestones and dates that are identified for a project implementation.

IRR (Internal Rate of Return)—Rate at which the present value of a series of investments is equal to the present value of the returns on those investments.

KPI—A KPI, or Key Performance Indicator, is an operational metric that is used to measure performance related to a project or a business objective. By assigning KPIs to people, accountability can be established within the organization so that project goals can be achieved. KPIs are measurable and obtainable and should be aligned with specific business objectives.

Milestones—A major stage or phase of a project that defines the project life cycle. Typically, multiple milestones are defined for a project.

NPV (Net Present Value)—Present value of an investment's future net cash flows minus the initial investment.

Payback Period—The length of time required to recover an initial investment through cash flows generated by the investment.

Project Success—A formula to measure the success of a project:

$$(\text{on time } + \text{ on budget}) \times \text{business value}$$

Simply put, business value is a multiplier that increases the overall success of a project: the more business value achieved, the more successful your project.

Project Status Report—A report periodically submitted by project managers to report current status and issues.

Project Value Booking—The ability to capture the actual values of the KPI metric while they occur or as they happen on a realistic and timely basis.

Risk Factors—The elements of risk for a particular project, grouped by category (delivery, technical, and business risk). The project risk factors are monitored via status reports that provide ongoing updates for each risk. In addition, risk factors are used to develop a risk mitigation plan, which helps ensure that there is a plan in place to minimize future risks and problems that may come up during the life cycle of the project.

Risk Mitigation—The action plan that is put in place to avoid identified risk factors for a given project.

Risk Ratings—A rating given to a risk factor based on a risk factor's impact on a project and the probability that the risk will actually occur.

ROI (Return on Investment)—Measurement to determine the financial return from an initiative that incurs cost.

Soft Benefits—Intangible benefits, which are hard to measure or cannot be calculated financially. Examples are customer satisfaction, efficiency, productivity, and regulatory or legal compliance.

Stakeholder—Stakeholders are people who are affected by and/or can influence change for a project. Anyone who is affiliated with a project can potentially have a positive or negative influence on the project. Typical stakeholders include:

External stakeholders: customers, suppliers, shareholders, government agencies, trade unions, consultants.

Groups: executive/steering committee, line management, specialists, support staff

Individuals: president, project sponsors/managers, process owners, team members, system users, department managers/supervisors

INDEX

accountability, assigning, 8, 74–75
   see also alignment/accountability,
     creating organizational; track-
     ing process, project perform-
     ance
action plan, creating an, 143–146
alignment/accountability, creating
     organizational
   accountability plan, stakeholder,
     141, 142
   action plan, creating an, 143–146
   baseline, establishing a, 41, 143
   change, the impact of, 137–138
   realigning the structure, 139–140
   rewards/incentives, 146–147
   skills, training for new, 138–139
   target goal, establishing the,
     143–144
approvers, project, 7, 21, 22
   see also case, the project business;
     influencers/supporters, busi-
     ness case; selection criteria for
     project approval

assessment and the project business
     case, initial, 23–26, 165–166
   see also key performance indica-
     tors; stakeholder management;
     tracking process, project per-
     formance

barriers, project, 26
body language, 131
bubble chart and comparing risk/
     reward, 63, 64
business case, *see* case, the project
     business
business risk, 43
business value, 2–3
   see also individual subject headings

cascading sponsorship network,
     98–99
case, the project business
   approval process, the formal,
     65–66
   assessment, initial, 23–26,
     165–166

ABOUT THE AUTHOR

For more than twenty years, Jeff Berman has developed a reputation for success by transforming organizations, and managing global projects for Fortune 500 companies such as Gillette, Johnson & Johnson, FMC, CertainTeed, and Cytec. He specializes in helping companies deliver measurable value from project investments by combining expertise in business processes with technology implementations.

Mr. Berman is currently Vice President of PM tec, Inc., a leading project management consulting firm focused on training and consulting for advanced project management systems and processes. Prior to PM tec, Mr. Berman was Vice President of ValueCurve Technologies, Project Solutions Practice Leader for PwC Consulting and IBM, and was Vice President for DTI's U.S. Consulting practice.

Mr. Berman holds an M.B.A. and a B.S. in Industrial Engineering from Northeastern University. He is a sought-after speaker and thought leader in project performance management, change & stakeholder management, and business case development. His keynote speaking events have included: Project Management Institute, American Production Inventory Control Society, New England Summit of Project Management, Mid Atlantic Project Summit, as well as many Fortune 500 client conferences.

He has authored several white papers, published articles, and training books including: *3 Steps to Project Success; Portfolio Management Critical Success Factors, Project Management Boot Camp, Business Case Boot Camp, and Stakeholder Management Best Practices*.

He can be reached at: projectvalue@pmtec.com or www.pmtec .com.